ADHD:
Strategic Parenting
From Tactical to Practical

By Terry James Gingras, Ph.D.

ADHD:
Strategic Parenting
From Tactical to Practical

ADHD: Strategic Parenting Series Book 1

© 2016 Terry James Gingras, Ph.D.

Published by Adriel Publishing

www.adrielpublishing.com

Edited by Karol H. Clark & Elizabeth A. Lawless

Printed in the U.S.A.

ISBN: 978-0-9971225-2-7

www.ADHDStrategicParenting.com

Dedication

To my loving and supportive wife, Shari, without whose support and encouragement this project would likely never been completed, I love you and I lack the words to tell you how much I value your contributions.

To my children – Erin, Nathan and Brian – my warmest thanks. You've taught me more about child rearing than any course I ever took or any book I ever read. I'm amazed and proud as I watch your lives develop. I love you very much.

Table of Contents

Introduction

Parenting is easily the most difficult thing an adult does. At the best of times it is still more complicated than anything you do vocationally, socially or recreationally. At the worst of times it is the most ego deflating activity an adult can experience. And this is the case with the so-called "normal" kid who has no diagnosable conditions. If your child has been diagnosed with attention deficit hyperactivity disorder, parenting becomes even more complicated.

Lots of veteran parents of these children will tell you the parenting a child with attention deficit disorder is a life and mind altering experience. These children are challenging. They're particularly challenging if you are the parent who doesn't also have attention deficit disorder. These children think differently. They have different issues with emotional control. They have huge problems with time management and organization. They're constantly forgetting shoes, homework or clothes, and the equipment they need for school, sports or lessons. Their concept of time is totally different. They honestly believe that a project that was supposed to take all month can be done in a half hour the night before it's due. They also believe that it's perfectly appropriate to spend two or three hours looking out the window rather than doing homework.

Perhaps it's due to their problems with attention, but these children see and react to the world in different ways. At their best they're incredibly creative and funny. They think about things in more detail and with a different context. That is why people with ADHD are seen as being creative. At their worst, however, they don't seem to see the obvious, particularly the consequences of their behavior. Parenting these children is a constant attempt to maintain control instead of them. It is frequently frustrating and discouraging. However, it is not hopeless. As mentioned previously, it is definitely a challenge but it can also be incredibly rewarding.

I was introduced to the world of ADHD when my youngest son was born. I already had two older children who were doing well and I thought I had this parenting thing under control. I was also a clinical psychologist who is supposed to know all about things like parenting. I was pretty confident about handling this new arrival. My first inkling that this experience might be a little different was when I found him hanging by one hand from the back of a full sized rocking chair. I have no idea how he got there, especially since he was not yet walking. He was quite content and totally unaware that a rocking chair could tip over backwards at anytime. As time went on, my wife and I found our youngest in many unusual situations, most of which were physically dangerous, but also suggested a high degree of coordination. Initially, I just thought he would probably end up a gymnast and let it go at that.

I was also aware, but dimly, that our home was in a higher state of disruption since his arrival. Our family was physically active with lots of sports and recreational activities so I just assumed that he was a little more active than his older brother and sister. Then he started school. He had difficulties almost from the start. He was not oppositional or mean or angry. He was just more active than most and had a harder time staying on task. He seemed to get bored much faster than his peers. Fortunately, he was a charmer. His teachers, even the ones who had problems with him tended to like him. While this was a good thing to some extent it also slowed us down in terms of getting help.

When the teacher is giving you mixed messages about your child, it is difficult to be sure if there's a problem or not. Maybe he's just a typical boy. Maybe he's just a little more active than most. There are all sorts of rationalizations, but eventually it becomes clear that something is not quite right. Finally, we decided that we had to get him evaluated. We had to know exactly what was going on and how to treat it. At this point in time I was principally an adult psychologist. I did not treat children. Frankly I thought a psychologist treating kids was a generation late. As a result, I didn't know what I needed to know to help my own son. The good side of this is that I had the resources and the knowledge to learn what I needed to learn. I went from not knowing much about ADHD to diagnosing and treating it as a major part of my practice. The purpose of this book is to help parents go through the process of diagnosis, treatment and parenting and have it be a whole lot easier than it was for me.

This book will provide needed information as well as some reassurance. I have written this book based on my 30+ years of experience working with ADHD children and their parents.I have chosen to emphasize the role of strategic parenting in dealing with these children. Because my son is now an adult, I have a broader concept of successful parenting than I had when he was young. Back in those days I just wanted to make him do what I wanted him to do. And indeed, many books on ADHD are mostly about discipline. I believe now that this is the wrong focus. I will explain in future chapters what I see is a more reasonable approach for long-term success. My main assumption is that the best result of successful parenting is a responsible adult. Not necessarily an obedient adult, but a responsible adult. This adult must have a reasonably positive self image. This does not mean that he has never heard a discouraging word, it just means that those aren't the only words he has heard. So welcome aboard, thank you for reading this book and I hope you find it helpful.

For the benefit of easier reading I am going to refer to the child in future chapters as he with the understanding that you might be raising a her, but the strategy still applies.

Chapter 1: So What the Heck is Strategic Parenting?

If you have a child with ADHD, your parenting skills are going to be challenged. There is no such thing as one trial learning with an ADHD child. They will not merely go along with you because you're the parent. They will not obey you just because you're the parent. They will also be on the lookout for any inconsistency in your parenting techniques and will take full advantage of any disagreement between you and your spouse.

There are plenty of parenting programs out there in the publishing world. The problem I have with most of them is that they are primarily tactical. By that I mean they're designed to help you win the immediate argument usually by utilizing the behavior modification techniques of BF Skinner. At their simplest, these techniques basically consist of punishing the behavior you don't want and rewarding the behavior you do want. Unfortunately, there is no context within which you're supposed to operate. There's nothing to tell you how much punishment is enough. There's also nothing that tells you when you shouldn't punish. I've seen families in my private practice that have gone more than a little bit overboard in terms of punishing their child by removing everything the child loves or likes until the child is sleeping on a mattress on the floor. They had no toys in the room and the door had even been taken off the hinges and removed. Unfortunately, this did not improve the child's behavior. Instead he stubbornly resisted any direction these parents gave.

Before I go much farther, there are a couple definitions we should review.

1. Tactical: According to Webster's New World dictionary, this was originally a military term referring to the science of arranging and managing military force in action or before the enemy. Tactics and tactical thinking are short term, intending to win the immediate situation whatever the cost. Now this term is used commonly in business and in most organizations, profit or nonprofit.

2. Strategy: This is the science of planning, directing large-scale operations; skill in managing and planning. This is another term that was originally primarily military but is now used in most large organizations.

The biggest difference between tactical and strategic thinking is that strategy wins you the war while tactics win you the battle. So strategic parenting is an approach to raising children that is future outcome oriented. That is, it is focused on the long-term, basically on the person you want your child to become. The strategic parent always is focused on the long-term, on the ultimate outcome. This focus is what gives you the context to help you decide whether to take action or not and how far to go with punishment.

The most important thing to remember is that being a parent means that your job is to train, nurture and mentor your child into an adult who's ready to enter the adult world and take adult responsibilities. Your job is not necessarily to teach your child to make the neatest bed or have the cleanest room or to get to bed at the exact prescribed time. That does not mean that you may not spend some time teaching and encouraging these things, but it's important to remember that these are not the primary lessons you want your child to learn. In the course of this program we are going to emphasize five major areas.

These five major areas are Preparation, Planning, Managing, Leading and Mentoring.

1. Preparation is the first stage of strategic parenting and involves recognizing that your ADHD child is different and special in the things that work with his or her neuro-typical siblings may not work with him. This is the part where you learn what you're dealing with. You have to find out everything you can find out about attention deficit disorder. You need to know what it is, a neurologic condition and how it affects children in general causing difficulties in time management, organization and emotional control. This is also where you consider your child's strengths and weaknesses. You must also decide what your goals are and here I mean long-term goals. What kind of an adult are you trying to train?

2. Planning involves getting your life and your family's lives in order to better deal with your ADHD child. You have to become aware of your favorite bad emotion, the one that keeps popping up and causing you difficulties because it is also going to cause difficulties with your child. You also need to be aware of your spouse's favorite bad emotions. You need to be aware of how the two of you interact when it comes to parenting. Specifically, do you support one another or do you cut one another down in the eyes of your child. This is also where you look at your household routines. ADHD children need an organized world with predictable routines. Does that describe your household?

3. Managing involves what you do to move your child towards the goals you've established for him. How will you move them towards your goals for him? How are you going to build his self-esteem? How are you going to ensure that the directions you give are followed? How are you going to ensure that he sees you as powerful in his life?

4. Leadership is the next phase. As the parent or parents, it is your job to lead your family confidently through the transformation from child to adult. You understand that your behavior is infinitely more powerful than what you say in teaching your child about the world. For instance, if you want him or her to be responsible about drugs and alcohol but you get a little tipsy every night because "work is so stressful", guess which is stronger, your behavior or your lecture? Leadership involves recognizing that your authority stems from your ability to influence your family because of your knowledge, skills, character, abilities, personality and, of course, your relationship. I am not referring to a power relationship. Rather, I am referring to a collaborative relationship. This won't be an issue for you unless you abuse your position. Remember, fussing never wins. There is such a thing as too many corrections as well as corrections given absentmindedly. I've been in session with families in which one parent or the other tried to correct their child's behavior literally every 10 seconds! Who could put up with that? And what do the kids do? The same thing we would all do. They quit listening.

5. Mentoring is the final stage of the strategic parenting process. As a parent, you are many things, but you are certainly a mentor to your child. This means you are a teacher with a specially privileged position. All parents are mentors to their children, but for ADHD children, there are some special areas that must be covered. We will talk about those and suggest some effective ways to manage them and implement them into your daily routine.

POINTS TO REMEMBER
- ADHD is a neurologic condition
- It is inherited
- The heritability index in 85% (very high)
- ADHD is characterized by decreased frontal lobe activity
- There is no difference between ADD and ADHD
- ADHDers have difficulties with time sense (awareness of the passage of time)
- ADHDers have problems with time management
- ADHDers have problems with organization
- ADHDers have problems with working memory (keeping information in awareness until they get the job done)
- ADHDers have problems with control of the attention process

Chapter 2: Preparation

As I have already emphasized and as you probably already know, parenting an ADHD child is more complicated and difficult than parenting a neuro-typical child. As a result, preparation is also more complicated and difficult. The first and the most obvious preparation is to learn about attention deficit hyperactivity disorder. Probably the first thing to learn is that there's no difference between ADD and ADHD. The fact that there are two terms says more about the kind of committees that design diagnostic systems than about the actual disorders. You will find that, in general, mental health professionals use ADHD, while pediatricians and family practice doctors tend to use ADD.

The most important thing to remember is that either term is used indiscriminately and does not indicate any more or less about your child's condition.The second thing to learn about ADHD is that it is a neurologic disorder. There is actually something physically different about the brain that results in ADHD. It is generally accepted that the prefrontal cortex of the brain is relatively under-active in ADHD children. The prefrontal cortex is the largest area of the brain and has to do with executive functioning, control of attention, working memory and sense of time. The major problem with understanding ADHD as a neurologic condition is that it causes behavioral problems. The inability to concentrate, difficulty starting tasks, difficulty finishing tasks, the apparent lack of memory and the inability to understand how much time it takes to get things done are all related to frontal lobe functioning.

ADHD is inherited. ADHD has an 85% heritability index which is incredibly high. It means that it is highly unlikely that only one child in an extended family has ADHD. It is probable that there are several relatives who also have ADHD, whether or not it has been formally diagnosed. If no one else in the family has been diagnosed, look to relatives that barely made it through high school but are now successful in business or are addicted to various recreational substances. These are the family members who would likely be diagnosed if formally evaluated. This should go without saying, but ADHD is not caused because mom ate too many donuts during the pregnancy or too many candy bars or snuck a couple of glasses of wine. It is an inherited, neurologic condition, period.

Also, diet did not cause ADHD and diet will not cure ADHD. However, ADHD kids tend to be more sensitive to blood sugar changes than the average child. So if you send your child off to school fueled with toaster waffles and Cap'n Crunch, expect to have a call from your child's teacher. Food's that are primarily simple carbohydrates such as those with a lot of sugar and white flour will cause a sudden spike in blood sugar that is uncomfortable for the body resulting in a rapid insulin spike which lowers the blood sugar level very rapidly. This results in extremely low blood sugar. Either really high or really low blood sugar is uncomfortable and increases irritability. It also causes difficulties with concentration and impulsivity.

For some reason medication is a major issue with ADHD parents. Although medications, particularly stimulants, are more than 85% effective for individuals with ADHD with relatively few side effects, the internet is full of horror stories about them. The internet is also full of helpful hints on all sorts of "Natural" treatments for ADHD. The truth is that none of these treatments have been researched and proven.

So parents of ADHD children, by all means, do the research. Read about ADHD. Read about medications. Read about alternative treatments. But don't let your logic and your wishes get confused. A treatment has to be proven before it's a treatment. Otherwise, it's just a way for some Norwegian fisherman to make a little extra money selling expensive fish oil. As Russell Barkley, PhD, arguably the best researcher on all topics related to ADHD said during a workshop in Richmond Virginia, "for any other disorder, if a treatment (stimulant medication) were as effective with as few side effects, it would be considered medical malpractice not to prescribe it."

So learning about the science involved in ADHD is a major part of preparing to be an effective strategic parent. The next and perhaps most obvious thing to be prepared for is to know what the evaluation process was for your child that resulted in their ADHD diagnosis. ADHD is a tricky diagnosis. There is no one test that confirms the diagnosis. There is certainly no blood test or CAT scan or x-ray that confirms the diagnosis. Unfortunately, there are all sorts of professionals with all sorts of levels of training who are making the diagnosis.

Probably the weakest diagnostic procedure is just an interview with no testing, no behavioral observations and an extremely short interview. The next weakest diagnostic procedure adds an 18-question the symptom checklist and that's it.

Because ADHD has symptoms that can be confused with other diagnostic categories, your clinician needs to test in those categories to rule them out. For instance, ADHD and anxiety problems are known to have overlapping symptoms. So a good evaluation requires evaluation of anxiety as well. For a thorough evaluation you have to be able to rule out anxiety, depression, learning disabilities and low IQ.

MY EVALUATION PROCEDURE

The following is the procedure that I use evaluating ADHD. First, I do a 45 to 50 minute interview with the parents, sometimes with the child, sometimes without him. The parents are given behavior observation forms – one set for them and one set for the teacher – that are to be brought back on evaluation day. Some of the forms are merely symptom checklists but I also include a reasonably complete psychological form that addresses issues such as anxiety, depression, anger and so on.

On evaluation day, the child spends 3 to 4 hours being evaluated with psychological and neuropsychological measures. Obviously, we test *attention and concentration* using both what is called a continuous performance test and more traditional neuro-psychological measures of attention and concentration. We assess *memory and learning for both verbal and visual information*. I am particularly fond of list learning tests because they allow us to measure the effect of distractibility on learning and memory. We test *language*, principally what is called fluency. Fluency involves generating word lists. Sometimes the child is given a category cue like name all the animals you can and sometimes a letter is given like name all the words you can think of that start with F but are not somebody's name. We address *visual-spatial processing such as spatial analysis and spatial construction*. We usually include measures of *fine motor control*. We administer an *IQ test* to determine intellectual level. The last category we usually include are *measures of psychological distress, principally anxiety and depression*.

This is a reasonably comprehensive evaluation. With such an evaluation, we will be able to rule out learning disabilities, anxiety problems, depression and limited intellectual ability. What is left is ADHD.

It should be noted that ADHD co-varies with all of the above categories. It is thought that the anxiety and depression stem directly from the ADHD. This principally starts in school. The anxious child just knows that he is going to make a mistake and get into trouble he is just not sure when. The depressed child is typically deciding that his academic difficulties are because there's something wrong with him.

It is vitally important that you get an adequate evaluation of your child. You should also receive a detailed feedback session and a copy of the report telling you what your child's diagnosis is and what his strengths and weaknesses are. This is vital for planning your child's education and even his future.

With an adequate evaluation, you can also evaluate treatment options. ADHD is normally distributed, that is, you can have a little bit of it or you can have a lot of it. If you've got a whole bunch of it, you're probably going to need to be on medication. If you've got only a little, you may be able to work with behavior modification techniques only or computerized cognitive retraining or neuro-feedback.

The other area of your child's life that is helped by an adequate evaluation is dealing with the school system. In general, children with ADHD are not eligible for an IEP. An IEP – an individualized education plan – is normally indicated only for children with learning disabilities. Occasionally, a school system will grant one to a child with ADHD. An ADHD child is eligible for a 504 plan. A 504 plan, so-called because it is specified in section 504 of the Americans with Disabilities Act, specifies the accommodations that your child will receive. The accommodations are designed to minimize the negative effects of ADHD on your child's education. Typical accommodations include preferential seating near the front of the room, testing in a distraction free environment, extended time for testing. There are other options available and you should become thoroughly familiar with this procedure before dealing with your child's school. (see the resources appendix for a list of information sources.) A specific source of information about your child's rights under federal law comes from a site called – www.wrightslaw.com. The site is run by Pete Wright, a lawyer who specializes in education law. He also happens to have ADHD and a learning disability. This site provides a wealth of free information on dealing with your child's school system.

So now that you have gotten a meaningful evaluation of your child that has confirmed the diagnosis of ADHD, you should also receive information on his strengths and weaknesses in processing information. Is he primarily a visual learner or a verbal learner? Or, is he one of those kinesthetic learners who only learn with hands-on experience?

In general, you want to know his cognitive strengths and weaknesses. You should be given a lot of statistical information telling you how good or how bad each of these areas are. You should also receive recommend-ations as to whether or not your child should be further evaluated for a learning disability. There is frequently a significant overlap between ADHD and learning disability.

COGNITIVE ABILITIES

The following is a list of cognitive abilities. Obviously any area could be a strength or a weakness.

Attention
1. Sustained attention—paying attention to repetitive (boring) tasks
2. Selective attention—basically sustained attention in a distracting environment
3. Alternating attention—having to switch attention back and forth from one category of information to another
4. Divided attention—all of the above. Paying attention in distracting environment and having to do a mental

manipulation to the information (perhaps a mathematical calculation)

Memory
Memory is very complicated. There is both the source of the information to be remembered (verbal vs. visual is the most common differentiation) and the type of information. The following categories are generally accepted:

1. Episodic or Personal memory—memory for things that have happened to an individual. Who was your first grade teacher? Where did you grow up?
2. Procedural memory—memory for things that become habitual. What shoe do you put on first? How do you fire up your X-Box?
3. Semantic memory—This what most people think of as memory, the ability to form new memories. What did you learn in school today?
4. Working memory—this is not information you plan to remember, just information you want to have in awareness until the job is done. Example: "Go to your room. Change your clothes. Make your bed and put your toys away." (ADHDers have a horrible time with this one.)

Language
Language is another very complicated area with no consistently accepted characteristics.

1. Receptive language/reading—understanding the written word
   a) Phonological processing—being able to hear the sounds the letters represent
   b) Decoding—being able to sound out words

c) Reading comprehension—a complicated process involving decoding the sounds the letters represent and holding the information in working memory long enough to understand the sentence or paragraph.

2. Receptive language/spoken—understanding what is said to an individual.

a) Decoding—automatic process of hearing and understanding the spoken. Some people, without hearing problems, have trouble doing this fast enough to maintain normal conversation.

b) Comprehension—being able to retain and understand what is said

3. Expressive language/written—being able to express one's ideas in the written word. There can problems with fine motor control or cognitive difficulties that interfere.

4. Expressive language/ spoken—the ability to express one's thoughts with the spoken word. Can be problems that are physical, psychological or cognitive.

Visual-spatial

Visual-spatial involves the processes of spatial analysis and spatial construction.

1. Spatial analysis—being able recognize and discriminate between different patterns and symbols. An example is being able to rapidly identify the different letters and numbers. It also involves being able to retain locations in space such as where is your desk?

2. Spatial construction is being able to construct or draw different symbols and patterns.

Executive functioning

Is the complex area involving reasoning, problem solving, control of emotions and judgement.

1. Concrete operations—solving problems the way you were taught to solve problems.
2. Fluid reasoning—solving problems in a novel situation in which there is no learned solution
3. Emotional regulation—being able to control emotions, for instance being irritated rather than mad.
4. Judgement—being able to weigh the positives and negatives of different courses of action and select an appropriate solution.

And finally the report should tell you about your child's psychological or emotional state. There is a significant overlap between ADHD and both anxiety and depression. The anxiety is related to your child's belief that he is eventually going to screw up and it will be bad when he does. The depression is related to the belief that "something must really be wrong with me, maybe I'm stupid" because he believes "I can't do anything as easily as the other kids". In my experience, often when the ADHD is effectively treated with both medication and psychotherapy, the anxiety and depression are resolved. This is not a guarantee, but it does frequently occur.

COMPONENTS OF COMPREHENSIVE ADHD EVALUATION

- Measure of intellectual ability
- Screening measure of reading ability—reading recognition test
- Continuous Performance Test—measures control of the attention process and impulsivity

- Measures of higher levels of attention
- Measure of verbal learning and memory (I prefer a list learning test)
- Measure of visual memory (I prefer a design copy task that gives information on spatial analysis and spatial construction ability as well as frustration tolerance)
- Fluency tasks-I use verbal fluency requiring generating lists of words in a timed interval. Tells about verbal processing as well as focus.
- Personality Testing—specifically looking at anxiety and depression
- Behavioral observation forms—For parents and teachers. I use both the simple symptom checklists and a more comprehensive measure that tells about ADHD behaviors as well as other psychological problems

If your child has a particularly fragile psyche, this will be something you'll want to take into account, when dealing with him. If he's depressed, you will want to build up his self-esteem. This is not done by being phony and praising him every time he ties his shoes. Rather, look for times when he has shown persistence and tried again after he's initially failed at something.

If he is anxious, particularly if he is starting to show signs of becoming compulsive and rigid, teach him to see the learning potential in any failure experience. You'll want to be saying things like "what did you learn when you try to do that?" Remember, we all fail and the best of us learn from our failures and eventually become successful. When you fail, particularly if you fail spectacularly, the last thing you want to hear is "what the heck is the matter with you? Couldn't you tell that that wouldn't work?"

You've gotten a decent evaluation. You know your child's cognitive strengths and weaknesses and psychological strengths and weaknesses. These are the things that objective testing tells you.

Now you need to add the subjective information that you know.

> What does your child do well?
> What does he enjoy doing?
> Is he really good at sports? Music? Art?
> Technology? Leadership?

You should have some idea of what he's really good at from your years of observation. You might have to work a little bit to recognize these skills and abilities. Knowing these may give you insight and valuable information as to your child's future.

=====================

My ADHD Child

For instance, my ADHD child is now a jewelry designer in New York City. This is not anything I would've planned for him. We have no family history of anybody in the jewelry business. The family bloodlines are French, Welsh, Scottish and English! What do we know about diamonds? My dad was a golf pro. My mother was a special education teacher. My father-in-law was a doctor. My mother-in-law did taxes. No jewelers. No precious gem evaluators. No designers.

I thought my son's greatest strengths were in sales or public relations. I still remember the time when he sold all of his older brother's Little League candy, just for fun. My older boy, at this stage in his life, was a shy, quiet typical middle child. He, of course ,encouraged his little brother and his little brother, of course, charged him a week's allowance.

My son was always bargaining and trading with his friends. He'd come home with a new toy and explain that he traded his friend for it. He was really very good at what he did and rarely did he come out on the short end of a trade. So I thought this would be his place in life.

His next business (that I knew about) was selling veggie burritos at rock concerts. He'd spend two days making these things and would be sold out within two hours. He made a lot of money.

His next step was trading in crystals, also at rock concerts. Apparently the folks who attend rock concerts are really into crystals. They apparently attribute all sorts of powers, such as healing, to different kinds of crystals. My youngest started developing on eye for crystals and became more knowledgeable about them.

Next step – semi precious stones. He has now moved into the world of rubies sapphires, amethysts and other stones with which I'm not familiar. Soon, he was traveling all over the country, buying and selling semi precious stones. Again, he was developing some knowledge and an eye for quality. He is also making pretty good money.

Then he takes a gemologist course at a well-known gemology school. It's a demanding six month course. He passes it on his first try while many of his classmates had to repeat the course.

I won't bore you with any more details except to tell you that he also took courses in design and jewelry making. Like I said before, I would never have thought that my child would end up as a jewelry designer. I also did not stand in his way. I tried to *encourage any positive movement in his life even if I was not entirely comfortable with it.*

=====================

So for all of you, become aware of your child's strengths and weaknesses. Encourage them to explore their abilities, even if you're not 100% comfortable with them. Remember there are people in the world who make a living playing video games.

GOALS

The next thing to consider is your goals for your child. As you see from my story, you can't necessarily pick their career. Rather, you should be thinking in terms of the kind of personality traits you'd like your child to have.

For me, integrity is the single most important characteristic an adult can have. If you don't have that, I don't want to be around you. Other important characteristics include loving and caring for your family, being persistent (or ornery as my grandmother used to term it) and being honest. These are not the only characteristics I value, but they are probably the most important.

The interesting thing about these characteristics is that parents teach these by what they do more than by what they say. My youngest son still talks about the time when we found a wallet in the men's bathroom at a subway station in Washington, DC. The wallet was loaded, literally bulging with money. He thought I had lost my mind when I turned it over to two subway guards. Later he started to understand it. And now, although he is in his 30s, he still remembers that story.

You also get to teach your child some of the fun stuff, the things that you really enjoy. It could be:

- sports,
- music,
- art,
- hiking,
- mountain biking,
- kayaking,
- surfing and
- on and on.

These are the fun things but they also are valuable for a child who has difficulties with organization, time management, attention and concentration. All of these activities and many more that I did not name require a certain amount of organization, time management, attention and concentration.

Your child will consider becoming more organized and careful after hiking for a couple of hours with his mess kit poking him in the back because he didn't bother to pack properly. He'll become more careful after a couple of hours of paddling his kayak without anything to drink because he left his water bottle in the car. The wonderful thing about these lessons is that the consequences are natural. You, as the parent, did not have to do anything and still, the lesson is learned.

For the latest news or additional information visit my website at www.AHDHStrategicParenting.com.

POINTS TO REMEMBER

- Have a set of character goals for your ADHD child—honest, integrity, perseverance.
- Observe and collect your child's strengths and weaknesses, not just the academic ones. Is he a good athlete, musician, video gamer, leader, designer?
- Get a proper evaluation—An 18-question rating scale that you complete in your pediatrician's office is not adequate.
- Get a detailed feedback session from the evaluating psychologist. Get a copy of the report. Make sure you understand it.
- Don't be afraid to schedule multiple feedback sessions until you can understand the causes of your child's difficulties and his measured strengths and weaknesses.

Chapter 3: Planning

Now, you have a good evaluation. You know your child's cognitive strengths and weaknesses. You know his psychological strengths and weaknesses. And you've looked at the strengths and weaknesses you see every day. You kind of know, right now, what to expect from your child.

I want to encourage you to take a long-term perspective dealing with your ADHD child. Focus on where you want your child to be when he's 18 or 20 or 25. Then look at where he is right now. Don't spend a lot of time thinking about where he should be. This is largely useless and counterproductive. Don't consider where his big brother was at the same age. Don't even consider what his peers are like. This does not do you any good. You have to start from where your child is and go from there. Also, understand that ADHD children are typically about three years behind their peers in terms of emotional development. This means you should expect them to be a little bit behind. Again, it doesn't really matter what your expectations are. Where your ADHD children are is where they are. And that's where you have to start from.

For example, if they have trouble with time management, you have to teach awareness of time passage and how much work you can get done in a given time period. If they have trouble with organization, you have to teach some organizational skills. Remember, there are many different organizational styles and ways of being organized. Find one that fits your child. Realize that it may not be the one that works for you. Be flexible.

Always remember – long-term perspective – how you want them to turn out? What kind of people you want them to be?

Now your job is to do everything you can to get them the help, support and space they need to explore their options. Ideally, they explore those options while still showing the characteristics you want them to develop. In my case, I value integrity above almost every other characteristic. Therefore, I allowed my child a great deal of space to experiment with different lifestyles, career choices and training as long as he was truthful and kept his word.

CHARACTER STRENGTHS

Consider which ones you value the most.
- Honesty
- Curiosity
- Kindness
- Fairness
- Creativity
- Perseverance
- Self-control
- Humor

With that value, honesty and integrity as my main focus, everything else was secondary. More important than grades, more important than cleaning his room, more important than being punctual. These other things become controlled by the environment eventually anyway. The integrity is something I could help develop and reinforce.

PLANNING PHASE

The next step is the planning phase. With an ADHD child you can't just react. If you do, unless you have the personality characteristics of a saint, you will almost certainly blow it. You will either get angry and overreact which will result in a yelling and screaming match with your child or the other extreme is that you will wimp out, because you're not sure what you should do. This is also not effective. As a matter of fact, of the two, this is probably the worst because it teaches your child that he can get away with poor behavior. You then end up with an entitled child who thinks the rules don't apply to him. He may also think that you've given up on him.

These are two extremes and you just don't want to go there. So the first thing you need to do is become more self-aware. You have to know what your tendencies are. How do you tend to respond emotionally when things are not going your way? How do you tend to respond physically? What are you thinking at these times?

Do you tend to become angry, loud and even more directive? Or do you tend to become anxious and indecisive and not do anything? A more general question is – what is your favorite bad emotion? In other words, what is the emotion you most frequently feel even in situations that don't immediately call for anger or some other emotion.

For instance, I'm retired Air Force officer. My father was a drill sergeant in the Army. Guess what discipline style I learned? The basics I learned not at my father's knee but over his knee, were that the order was given once and it was to be obeyed instantly. There was no talking back. There was no arguing. Any negotiation would be done after you did what you were told.

Now, as a well-trained psychologist, I was gentler and a good bit quieter than my father, but the basic expectation of immediate compliance was still there. Honestly, there were no particular problems with my first two children. As a matter of fact, I thought I had that parenting thing under control. And then...well let's just say I learned a whole lot more from my third child then I did from the other two combined. My initial response was irritation, followed by frustration, followed by anger. I was not particularly prone to reacting physically, but it was pretty obvious when I was upset. With my third child, the bottom line was that I had to watch any display of anger. Not only was it ineffective in getting him to do what was asked, but he also tended to respond to anger by getting more and more agitated. He was an emotional barometer and reacted strongly to whatever the predominant emotion was in the room.

FAVORITE BAD EMOTIONS

One of the processes I often use is my Favorite Bad Emotions Test. It's designed to help you identify your favorite bad feeling, the one that causes you most of the trouble and distress in your life. Use it to get to know yourself (self-awareness) and your spouse.

The test is composed of 20 real life situations that we all have experienced. The situations don't necessarily cause any particular emotion. That's what you do. Read each situation and put a check mark in the box with the emotion you feel or would feel in that situation. At the end add up the checks for each emotion. You'll be able to tell what your emotional tendency is and what you need to watch out for when dealing with your ADHD child.

The test lists only the basic four emotions—anger, fear, sadness and guilt. All the other emotions—frustration, scared, irritable fit under one of these categories.

Once you have good self-knowledge, knowing your favorite bad emotion, and knowing how your child responds to this emotion then decide if it's helpful or not. Once you have done this, the next step is a tiny bit trickier. It's the question of what is your spouse's favorite negative emotion?

Since people rarely marry people who are exactly like themselves. We tend to marry people who are complementary rather than identical. For instance, two people were chronically angry aren't likely to last very long in a marriage. Therefore, it is likely that your spouse's favorite bad emotion is different from yours.

The question is, what exactly is that emotion and is it helpful in parenting situations with your child? For instance, if you get angry and your spouse gets fearful and tearful, how does this affect the interaction with your child?

Favorite bad emotions

How do you feel in each of these situations?

	Angry	Sad	Afraid	Guilty
1. Someone cuts you off while you are driving.				
2. Someone interrupts you when you are concentrating on something.				
3. Someone disagrees with you.				
4. Someone belittles you.				
5. Someone takes the last cookie, chip, meatball, hors d'ouvere, candy.				
6. A friend doesn't do what he/she promised.				
7. A co-worker/friend asks for help at the last minute, right before a deadline.				
8. A friend/co-worker wants you to take over a job they're responsible for.				
9. A friend criticizes you.				
10. You misplace something important.				
11. You forget an important appointment.				
12. The teacher calls about your child's behavior.				
13. A neighbor calls about your child's behavior.				
14. When your child gets upset about a consequence and yells, "It's not fair!" and throws a temper tantrum.				
15. An hour after you told him to turn it off, your child is still playing video games.				
16. The police knock on your door and tell you your son was spotted throwing rocks through the windows of an abandoned house.				
17. You spill your coffee all over your paperwork.				
18. You are parallel parking and you bump the car behind you.				
19. You are trying to return a Christmas gift and the shipping clerk says you can't without a receipt.				
20. Your spouse forgets your birthday.				
TOTAL				

What is your most frequent response?   Angry   Sad   Afraid   Guilty

The biggest question is – do you work together when you're disciplining your child? Are you on the same page and are you working towards the same goal? Or, are you constantly cutting each other off, arguing with each other and generally confusing the situation.

Parents need to be unified and consistent, particularly when they're dealing with an ADHD child. ADHD children are particularly observant and aware of the subtleties of human communication. If they spot discord, disagreement and lack of unity, they will take advantage and play you against each other. It's not malicious and it's not the sign of a budding psychopath, all children do it. ADHD children tend to be a little better at playing one parent against the other. This may be because they get more practice than other children since they tend to get in trouble more often.

Parents need to communicate with each other about how they plan to deal with their ADHD child. The first thing they need to do is agree on their common goals. My preference is let the goals be the big ones – integrity, honesty, persistence, self-esteem/confidence, love of learning. This may not be the same as your list but concentrate on those lifelong important goals. Picking up your socks and making your bed are not important lifelong. Hold that thought in mind and life with your ADHD child will be much better.

You need to understand that you can only work on a limited number of goals at one time. In fact, working on two or three goals is about the limit. Do not try to work on everything at once.

Also, keep your corrective comments to a minimum. I've seen families when one or the other parent is continuously correcting the child – "sit up straight, look at the doctor when you talk, quit fidgeting, be respectful and on and on and on." Literally, the child was receiving corrective comments several times a minute. Guess what? You don't have to be ADHD to rapidly tune out that kind of communication. If you are constantly correcting, your child is going to quit listening to you.

So part of being a strategic parent of an ADHD child is to be able to pick your battles. Know when to bite your tongue and when to comment. Keeping the strategic goals in mind at all times is very helpful in making these decisions. You'll find that doing less correcting of your child gives you more time to notice and make comments on the positive things your child does. We will discuss this principle in further detail later in this book, on but it is important in building confidence in your child that he hear more than negative comments all the time.

PARENT PREPARATION

- Emotional Control—know your tendencies and control them
- Know your spouses tendencies
- Work together-be unified and consistent
- Talk with each other ahead of time, plan ahead
- Limit the number of goals you're working on with your ADHD child at any one time
- Minimize critical comments
- Pick your interventions to times when they'll most likely succeed, not after the worst day of his life!

The next thing to be aware of, when you're planning, is your household routines. How does your household run? Is it well-organized and consistent so everyone knows what's going to happen when? Or is it chaos with everything being done at the last minute and people rushing around, upset and frustrated.

More than most children, an ADHD child, needs to have an organized environment. If everything is always done at the last minute with no warning and no plan, they will tend to get upset and frustrated. They will also take what they see and apply it to their own lives. If they don't see organization, they will be less likely to be organized themselves. If they see a lack of routine, they are not likely to develop routines of their own.

Always remember that what you show your child is far more important than what you tell them. Your child learns more from what you do than from what you say. That's the first point. Second, your ADHD child gets physically uncomfortable amidst chaos. Their solution to this discomfort is to go off and do their own thing. This makes them feel more comfortable. However, it probably makes you feel less comfortable.

So it is important that you have routines in your home. What time are meals? Who's going to be there? What time is homework done? When does he get to play? When can he watch TV? How much time does he get to play video games? When does he take a shower? Brush his teeth? What's the morning routine? Who gets the bathroom first? When do we do laundry? What are his chores? When is he supposed to do them?

Of course there are more parts to the routine then I have listed, but at a minimum, when your ADHD child comes home from school, he should know what the routine is. The routine should include some physical activity. Your ADHD child needs regular physical activity. Unfortunately, many schools no longer provide any physical activity during the school day. This is of course absurd but it is not the topic of this book. In addition to physical activity, he needs to have an established time to do homework. You have two main obstacles here. One, there are way more time wasters now than there used to be—video games on all different kinds of platforms, cell phones, tablets, computers. The other, is that children with ADHD tend to need more time than their peers to get the same amount of homework done. Finally, there tends to be far more homework than there used to be. So, it is important have an established routine for doing homework in an established location with a minimal amount of distractions.

Put your child in a room where you can see or hear the television and the homework session will never end. You need to have a quiet place with the minimum number of distractions. You also need some amount of supervision. This is provided by someone who can actually pay attention to the child and recognize when he is off target or needs help. This individual also doesn't need to be making constant comments.

This is a tricky situation. You need to have supervision so you can intervene when necessary, but you also need to watch out for encouraging dependency. If your ADHD child knows that you will step in and give him the right answer every time he acts a little frustrated, you will be doing his homework for the rest of his life. His job is to learn. Your job is to encourage him to do the work necessary to learn.

A STRATEGIC HOUSEHOLD

So, what does a strategic household look like? First, it is obvious that a strategic household is a family. That means that the family spends time together. They eat meals together. They celebrate together. They work together. They know that they depend on one another. They each make some contribution to help the family function. This means that everyone has chores that other people count on them to do. This includes your ADHD child. Don't give them a pass when it comes to chores because they have ADHD.

A strategic household has routines. There is a family routine for getting up in the morning and preparing for the day. As much as possible, families should eat breakfast together. Ideally, there is minimal time spent with time wasters such as TV and computers. Everyone knows what they have to do and when they have to do it. They need to have learned to help each other out if someone can't do their part of the routine.

Routines are also important at the end of the day. When the children come home from school, who is in the house waiting for them? What are they expected to do? In what order do they do exercise, play and homework? Routines have to be established for all these things. Routines are established over time. They will evolve and change as people grow and mature.

There has to be a routine for homework. What time should he start? Where does he do it? Who will help if he gets stuck? You have to answer all these questions and establish all these routines. The specifics will depend on the family members.

Older, more responsible children can reasonably expect to do their homework in their rooms. Sometimes though it may be more helpful to the family if they do their homework in a common area where the younger children are doing their homework. This way they can provide help for their siblings, both answering questions and providing a model for how to study.

There is also routine for the evening meal. There's a fair amount of research, in addition to my personal experience that suggests that the family should gather together to prepare and eat the evening meal together. Families that make this a regular routine tend to be more cohesive and work together better. This is a chance to keep up with how everybody's life is going. It's also a chance to share opinions and eventually discuss broader topics such as politics, economics, current events, cultural events, science and technology. Of course, this depends on the ages of the children and the interests of family members.

There also needs to be a routine for going to bed. When do we shower? Brush teeth? Go to bed? What's the bedtime routine? Does a parent read a story every night? What about prayers? Nightlight? Or not? The bedtime routine, especially for younger children, should be comforting and familiar.

An underlying core for a strategic household is a certain level of personal discipline in all the family members. The goal for all is to learn and develop. Anything that helps that is good. Anything that interferes with that process is bad. This brings us to a discussion of technology. Technology – cell phones, tablets, computers, the Internet – is not bad. As a matter of fact, technology is revolutionizing the world. It is impossible to be a participant in that world and not know how to use technology.

The problem is, like anything else from alcohol to peanut butter, you can use it or you can abuse it. As you look around our world, you can see there are many people who are abusing technology. You can tell because you never see anything but the top of their heads since they are so busy with their cell phones. I have seen some couples that I swear text each other in bed! I have also had as patients, some young people, mostly teenagers who have become so addicted to their video games that they quit going to school. I had one young patient who had to repeat a whole year of high school because he was so addicted to video games. He was a fairly clever young man and his father was a doctor. So this young man developed (or reported) vague physical symptoms to his father. His father, being a concerned parent as well as a physician, proceeded to order the million-dollar workup for his young son. This young man had x-rays, CAT scans and MRIs as well as blood tests and consultations with various specialists all to no avail. By the way, this young man also got to skip school because he was ill. As a result, he missed nearly an entire year of high school.

TECHNOLOGY CAN BE TRICKY

As a parent, it's important for your child to know how to use technology, but it is also important for your child to understand that there are limits. Unfortunately, the information on the Internet is endless. It just keeps coming at you. It's like trying to get a drink out of a fire hose. The pressure, the force is just too strong. The individual has to learn to regulate his consumption because the system, the Internet, is surely not going to provide less information.

Therefore, as a parent, you need to set and reinforce reasonable limits. This is especially tricky. Increasingly, your child needs access to a computer to do homework. From homework it's a simple click or two to get to your favorite video game. Still, reasonable limits are necessary, especially for your ADHD child. There are two reasons. One they are particularly attracted to the latest shiny object. Video games are perfect for ADHDers. They are fast, there's a lot going on and it's exciting. Perfect! Your child will happily play all day and all night if you let them. The other problem is that due to distractibility, it takes your ADHD child longer to do homework. Clearly video games and homework are a bad combination. You need to set limits and they need to be limits you can enforce.

The next characteristic the strategic household is consistent parents. Both parents are on the same page. They are working on the same two or three issues. They are consistent with their discipline and they follow through.

It is sometimes amazing to watch family interaction and see the number of times one parent will undercut the other. For instance, one parent will say something like "you know you're supposed to be doing this, so let's get on with it." The other parent will come in with all sorts of excuses as to why it's impossible for your child to do whatever it was.

Guess what happens next? Guess what you are teaching your child? Your child's being taught that it is okay to ignore one parent because the other parent will always come to the rescue. ADHD children are particularly sensitive to this sort of inconsistency. They will play one parent against the other constantly. The real problem is, you are teaching your child to ignore the rules. This almost always leads to very bad outcomes.

The stereotype is, the dad is always the big mean disciplinarian and the mother is always the apologist. This is not necessarily true. I remember one family with a teenage son who was ADHD. Dad was frequently gone on business trips and mom was left at home to deal with him. While dad was gone on one business trip, the son took the family car to visit a girlfriend in a distant city. He did this in spite of the fact that he was on academic probation and didn't have permission to drive the car, much less take it out of town. The mother, did not know where he was and was understandably frantic. The son returned the next day and acted as if nothing had happened. I saw the family two or three days later and not only had dad not backed up his wife's attempts at discipline, he had presented his son with a new car!!

Talk about undercutting your spouse and failing to teach your child the rules! This was about as blatant an example as I've seen in my career. The family dropped out of therapy sometime later. (I don't think it was anything I said.) The last I heard, the son tried to enlist in the Army and failed to complete boot camp.

If you tend to be the apologetic parent, you need to look at your own issues. Why do you have so much trouble imposing discipline on your child? What is it that gets in the way of realizing that teaching the rules is an important life lesson for your child? You really need to explore those issues. Are you afraid he won't love you? Do you feel guilty about being "mean"? Whatever's going on with you, you need to realize it is important to your child to learn there are certain limits and rules that everyone needs to follow. If you can't get comfortable with this concept, you need to look at your own issues and perhaps consider psychotherapy.

I don't say this to drum up business for the psychologist's union. I say this because I've seen the harm done to a young child by inconsistent parenting. The problem is, instead of training a responsible adult, you are training someone to ignore the rules. You're teaching them that there is no consequence to their behavior. Unfortunately, as they get older, society weighs in and starts enforcing its own consequences which are frequently more severe than any family's consequences. And if society doesn't cause difficulties, there are some natural consequences in life that start to cause difficulties.

If your child learns to ignore the rules and that there are no consequences to behavior, how is he ever going to get through school? How is he ever going to get through the difficult training involved in completing military boot camp or vocational training for a large company? How is he ever going to be disciplined enough to get through college?

Consistently enforcing a limited set of rules in a calm and measured way is the best way to teach your child self-discipline and responsibility. The hard work for the parents is consistently enforcing the rules. Believe me, it takes some effort to be consistent when you're tired after a long day or have other things on your mind, but the long-term reward is more than worth the effort.

FAMILY ATMOSPHERE

The next important thing in a strategic household is the family atmosphere. This is the feeling you get from families that do things together, eat meals together, discuss the activities of their days together. It may not seem like it but getting together at least every evening for dinner is vitally important. This is where you develop the family bond that lasts throughout life. This is where you learn that the families got your back and you've got theirs. Think of the Reagan family in the TV show, Blue Bloods. In spite of the fact that the children are all adults, they get together weekly for Sunday dinner to share what's going on in their lives. This is as it should be. Your child is not going to develop a sense of family bonding and responsibility eating Big Macs in his room while texting his friends.

You have to put in the time to develop a sense of family and understand that mealtime should not be discipline time. This is the time to share views, report on your activities, ask for advice and generally interact with other family members. It is not the time for constant discipline, constant belittling or constant criticism. It is a time to make connections, reinforce your child's interests and teach them how to discuss their life events with people who appreciate them.

The worst thing is when the evening meal becomes dreaded because somebody's always getting in trouble, being yelled at or being disciplined. This is not the time to vent your frustrations after a hard day at work. Ideally, you want people to look forward to the evening meal. Or, at least accept that it is a regular part of the day.

The last major component of a strategic household and perhaps one of the major components of strategic parenting as a whole is having a long-term perspective. As a parent, you have the most important job of your entire lifetime. Remember, at the end of life people are most concerned about family and friends. Very few are wishing that they had spent more time at work!

So, it is important for you to remember that you have young lives to shape and mold into responsible adults. This is your most important job. You must never forget that. No matter how much money you make or how many promotions you get, at the end of life you will be most concerned about your family – your children, your grandchildren and how their lives are going

You must constantly be looking long-term.

How is what I'm doing right now going to affect my child in the future? If I let them get away with this one, what are the long-term implications? Always keep in mind that there are a few core values that are extremely important. Some of these values vary from family to family but almost everyone is concerned about integrity and responsibility. You want your child to grow into an adult who is honest and does what they say they will do. Ideally, you also want a resilient child, someone who can take a loss, recover and keep going. Believe me, if your child has ADHD, they will have plenty of experience with making mistakes. The important thing is not to give up when things don't go the way they want, but to be able to learn, make corrections and continue on. If your child learns that, they will be successful in life. It's the kid who collects failures and gives up who will never succeed.

So as a parent, it's more important that your child tells the truth than that they pick up their socks or make their beds every day. Therefore, always focus on the long view and try not to sweat the small stuff.

CHARACTERISTICS OF A STRATEGIC HOUSEHOLD

- It is organized, there are established routines
- There is a morning routine- in what order are things done-showers, eating breakfast, getting dressed? Who goes first?
- There is an after-school routine—when is play time? When is snack time? When is homework done? Where?
- There is a bedtime routine-showers, tooth brushing, story-reading, prayers. When does it occur?
- Mealtimes are family times—meals are eaten together, with everyone helping out
- Mealtimes are times for discussion and learning about each other. They are not for dealing with the misconduct of the previous week.
- Technology is necessary don't let it be an evil. Set reasonable limits on the amount of time devoted to video gaming and social media.
- Parents know and accept that they are role models. If they are not calm and organized, they can't expect their children to be.

- Parents are consistent.
- Parents support each other.
- Parents make and enforce a limited set of family rules.

Chapter 4: Managing

You know that having a child with ADHD requires a lot of preparation and planning ahead. You know that you have to educate yourself about attention deficit disorder. You know that you have to look at yourselves, your spouse, your family, your family routines and habits and be familiar with the effect they have on your ADHD child. In addition, there are some strategies for managing your child's behavior and the difficulties that are commonly associated with ADHD.

If your child has ADHD, he will probably have difficulties with organization, time management, working memory, emotional ability and increased frustration. This leads to situations like having your child's teacher call and tell you that your child has not turned in homework in three weeks. You look in his backpack and find all three weeks worth of homework, crumpled up, torn and stained in the bottom under all his books. He doesn't necessarily see the problem.

Other issues with organization include not bringing the books home that he needs to do homework. This is especially a problem if your school system uses block scheduling. This is a particular nightmare for an ADHD child that has not one, but two different schedules that alternate. You may have a Monday schedule and a Tuesday schedule and you keep repeating all week long and guess what? On the next Monday your Tuesday schedule is your Monday schedule!

In addition, the class lengths are doubled and to make it even more interesting for your ADHD child, guess what the teachers do? The first half of the class is their normal lecture, the second half is group work. Guess what happens to your average ADHD child behavior after an hour and a half in the same class without a break? Of course, there's more behavioral acting out.

In short, the classes are too long. The schedule is too confusing and the stress on your child's limited organizational skills is huge. Some families resort to having separate book bags for each schedule. You can imagine what happens. Half the time, your child goes to school on Monday with his Tuesday bag and vice versa. And if you think you had problems getting them to turn in homework in elementary school and the schedule was the same all year long, your problems are multiplied by block scheduling.

Another issue of the school system is projects. Children with ADHD have time management problems. A major component of this problem is that they lack the innate sense of time passage and what can be done in a given unit of time. Bluntly, 10 minutes to them is the same as two hours. They just don't sense the difference. They honestly think that they can do a 10-page paper in 45 minutes that is due tomorrow. They just don't see the problem.

This is where getting reasonable accommodations, including flexible deadlines for projects is important. In my area, the school systems increasingly are emphasizing compliance over intelligence. In some courses, turning in the assignments on time is as important as your test scores! This is a definite gotcha for an ADHD kid. You know they're going to forget the assignment, forget to do the assignment or forget to turn in the assignment a certain percentage of the time. Since this is the result of a neurologic condition, it shouldn't be used against your child. Therefore another accommodation is that all assignments that are completed should be scored and given full credit.

Additionally, you should teach your child some basic time management skills. Teach them to use checklists and to do lists. A checklist is something you use for repeated behaviors like making sure you're ready for school. Give your child some responsibility and ownership for his school checklist and he will be more compliant. Don't just design it yourself and handed down to them. Give them some time to suggest what they need to do and when.

To-do lists vary from day-to-day and basically list what needs to get done. Teach them to make the list and then prioritize from what's most important to what's least important. That way, if everything doesn't get done, hopefully the most important things got done. Also, make it something that's helpful, a little bit of fun, not another chance to screw up. Don't get all compulsive and don't get all directive. Let them have input and be gentle about adding a bunch of extra things that are on your priority list.

====================

For example Timmy's Morning List

6:30 Get up when the alarm goes off
6:40 Go to bathroom
7:10 Brush teeth
7:20 Take shower
7:45 Get dressed, shoes, too
8:00 Eat Breakfast
8:20 Get coat (if necessary)
8:20 Get book bag (that you loaded up last night)
8:25 Double check your book bag
8:30 Go to bus stop

This is, of course, just an approximate schedule assuming the bus comes at 08:45 and the bus stop is 5-10 minutes away.

====================

Another variation on the to do list is the list of things that need to get done for a specific project. Say it's a report, you'd want to list resources (and with Google that should go very fast), set aside a certain amount of time to research, a set amount of time to outline the report and a certain amount of time to write and another block of time to edit. Actually write down a specific amount of time for each task. Then we introduce the ADHD lifesaver — a timer. In fact, a timer is useful for all of us. It sets some limits that we can see and hear. It tells us when we're done. We can tell how much longer we have to go. It's also remarkably good for those of us who have trouble starting any new project. This is actually a variation on a technique called the Pomodoro technique.

POMODORO TECHNIQUE

Pomodoro is Italian for tomato and the technique got its name because it used the kitchen timer that looked like a tomato. The top part, with the stem, was turned to set the time. Traditionally in the Pomodoro technique, you set the timer for 50 minutes. You agree that you will work for 50 minutes and then you get to take a break. If you want to, you can come back and do another 50 minutes or you can set it up so that 50 minutes a day is all you need to do. Your child may not be able to tolerate 50 minutes at first. So, start at 30 minutes until your child gets used to the technique. Then you can add time until you reach 50 minutes. Under no circumstances do you go for more than 50 minutes. At the 50 minute mark, everybody gets a break. Then, if necessary, you can go back to the table, reset the timer (the tomato) and start again. Let your child set the timer if at all possible. Also try to find a unique fun timer, not your usual sterile kitchen timer, but something that looks fun and interesting. The tomato is perfect, but you can get timers that look like animals and other more interesting things. Just make sure, it appeals to your child and doesn't immediately look like work.

Working memory is another issue for ADHD children. Working memory is a type of memory in which you don't really intend to remember the information; you just want to keep it in your awareness until the task is done. This can be as simple as getting up from the family room and going to the bedroom with two or three things in mind to do. If you do them all, your working memory is adequate. If you do one out of three you get a little bit of a problem. If you get to the bedroom and can't remember what you're doing there, you've got a major problem!

ADHD children typically have terrible working memories. This is why when you tell them to pick up the toys, put the dirty socks in the hamper and make their beds, you are lucky if they do one of these things. You are mistaken if you think they're doing it on purpose. Really, that may be as good as it gets. What this means for you is that you may have to use more frequent, but shorter to do lists. And, be tolerant, in this case, they are not challenging you. This is a really as well as they can do.

Poor working memory also causes problems in learning. When a neuro-typical child is learning something new, the new information is stored in working memory, long-term memory is accessed and the information is compared then it is consolidated, the new information with the old. If your working memory is weak and you keep forgetting what the new information is, it takes a lot longer to learn it. You have to keep reminding yourself of what the information is so that you can learn it. This is why ADHD children typically require more frequent repetition of the same information in order to learn new information.

It is important to remember that this has nothing to do with intelligence. Einstein reportedly had terrible working memory. Poor working memory also results in the so-called "scattered" child who remembers the information one day and acts like he never heard of it the next day! Frequent, brief repetitions are the key to helping an ADHD child learn new stuff.

You may have noticed, there are a lot of different techniques for helping your ADHD child. Most of them have to do with giving them visible feedback on the passage of time, teaching how to break projects into smaller simpler tasks and using frequent repetitions to consolidate learning.

The problem with having ADHD as a child is that you don't have enough life experience to compare your performance to what it could be. The simplest thing is to keep repeating the things that well-meaning, but not necessarily well-informed adults tell you about how you should "just try harder or just apply yourself or if you weren't so lazy or maybe you're just not very smart." These children know enough to know that they're not measuring up to the other kids. They have more trouble learning, they get into trouble more often, and they have more problems completing projects and homework. The tendency is to assume that I'm not smart enough, disciplined enough or responsible enough or I would get my stuff done in school and do well on tests and get all my homework done on time.

All the ADHD child knows for sure is that whatever it is he is doing now, it's not good enough. This leads to behavior problems. ADHD kids are not that great at tolerating frustration. When they are in a situation day after day in which they cannot win, seemingly no matter what they do, the frustration is chronic and spills over regularly. This is one of those times when having had a competent evaluation done is particularly helpful. Part of a competent evaluation is assessing intellectual ability and information processing ability in addition to assessing impulsivity, control of attention, distractibility and the other factors that make up ADHD. It's important for you to tell your child that he has the intellectual horsepower to do well in school. He just has more trouble than other kids staying focused.

I sometimes use as an example, a muscle car from the 60s with a 412 in.^{3} engine and a loose front end. The car has plenty of horsepower to go very fast and reach the destination rapidly but with a loose front end, it wobbles all over the road and therefore takes more time to get to the destination. My little boy patients particularly love this example. I still have to work on one for the girls.

ADHD is defined as a disability. It is specified in section 504 of the Americans with Disabilities Act and it causes a lot of difficulties for families and individuals. When you consider the difficulties academically, the difficulties in the vocational area, the number of divorces and broken relationships and the tendency to lubricate problems liberally with alcohol or drugs, ADHD causes a lot of problems. The way to adapt and adjust to ADHD is to treat it as a difference, like any other circumstance in life. For instance when I was a child I wanted to be sixth man for the Boston Celtics. Unfortunately, as a freshman in high school I was 5 foot two and weighed about 120 pounds. Clearly, the NBA was not for me. So, I had to adapt and adjust and learn to be happy kicking butt in pick up games in my neighborhood. I also learned that maybe a career as a professional athlete was not in my future, but I was a heck of a great reader.

You need to help your ADHD child to adapt and adjust to the fact that he has more difficulties staying focused than the average neuro-typical child. In my office, I routinely hand out a list of some of the famous people in the world who have ADHD.

===================

FAMOUS PEOPLE WITH ADHD

Having ADHD doesn't mean you have a handicap. As somebody once noted, "ADHD often endows children and adults with gifts such as creativity, intuition, imagination, and a sense of adventure."

Here is a partial list of people you might recognize:

Albert Einstein, scientist

Justin Timberlake, singer

Adam Levine, singer & musician "Maroon 5"

Mozart, musician

Michael Phelps, Olympic swimmer

John Lennon, musician "The Beatles"

Terry Bradshaw, football player & sports commentator

will.i.am, singer & musician "Black Eyed Peas"

Howie Mandel, actor, comedian & game-show host

Leonardo Da Vinci, artist & inventor

Whoopi Goldberg, actress & comedian

Karina Smirnoff, dancer on "Dancing with the Stars"

Danny Glover, actor

Shane Victoriano, baseball – Boston Red Sox

James Carville, political strategist

Stevie Wonder, singer & musician

Thomas Edison, inventor

Britney Spears, singer

Jim Carrey, comedian & actor

"Magic" Johnson, basketball & philanthropist

Walt Disney, film maker

Ryan Gosling, actor

Paris Hilton, socialite

Will Smith, actor & musician

Richard Branson, billionaire entrepreneur & adventurer

Babe Ruth, baseball

=======================

It is important that your child realizes that ADHD is not an insurmountable obstacle. You should also note that the competent evaluation I was talking about does not have a measure of motivation. Being motivated or ornery or stubborn, whatever you want to call it is more important to success in life than size, weight, beauty or brilliance. So it is important for you teach your child that he can be whatever he wants to be if he's willing to do the work.

I will briefly cover Parental Potency in this chapter although it is a big enough topic for another entire book. I have been working as a psychologist for a lot of years. I've seen hundreds, maybe thousands of families in various stages of dysfunctionality (that may be a new word, I just coined). The families that had the most difficulties tended to be ones in which the parents had essentially given up all power to their children. To the casual observer, this may look like what the child actually wants. But children need and want structure and support. The parents are supposed to provide this. If they don't, it's scary for the child, even the most defiant child as you can imagine. A structured and supportive environment is a safe environment. The child, at some level, knows that this means his parents have done a lot of work to keep him safe and that means that they love them.

Parents that have given up all their power have out-of-control children that overwhelm them. These children also worry and concern them. They know their children are headed in a bad direction and may not be able to recover. All the parental fears of drugs, pregnancy, school failure and dropout and jail or being killed are possible for these kids. It's like a stagecoach when the horses panic and stampede. If no one is there to establish control, the team of horses may go right off the cliff. That may sound a little melodramatic but it is realistic. Without direction and support, children, particularly ADHD children have a much higher likelihood of a bad outcome as adults.

When your child is born, you have all the power and you know it. You are bigger stronger, more experienced and you control all the resources. If not for you your baby doesn't get fed, bathed, diapered or vaccinated. In short, they don't survive. You may be concerned about the amount of responsibility, time and energy involved in raising a child but they don't scare you and they don't overwhelm you. But somehow, over time, if you don't use your power wisely, you'll find that you've given it up without even meaning to.

How do you give up power? You don't use your power to set limits and enforce the rules. You fight with your spouse over discipline issues. You set limits and then you don't enforce them. You threaten, but don't follow through. You ignore signs that something is amiss. You wait until it is too late to get involved in your child's life. You never establish a relationship with your child; never develop an awareness of your child's interests. You are always the critic, never a supporter.

You have the power but you have to use it. You have to set limits. You have to consistently support the limits. You keep a number of areas you're working on with your child to two or three at the most. You and your spouse are consistent and what rules you enforce and how you enforce them. You've done the work in private to establish your goals for your child. You never fight with each other in front of your child, particularly about discipline. You keep your criticisms to the minimum.

LASODA RULE

This last point is particularly important. I've seen families in which one parent or the other is continuously correcting the child. When you get that volume of criticism, the natural response is to develop tone deafness to that person. It's like "well I can't please her anyway, so I just won't listen." There is a principal in social psychology called the Lasoda Rule. It was originally based on the study of efficient workgroups. It was later expanded to include families and marriages. The study found that the most creative, highest functioning groups had a ratio of positive comments to criticism of approximately 4 to 1. That means that for every criticism there were four positive comments. This also applies to families with the same ratio being important. Interestingly, in marriages the ratio is slightly higher!

What the Lasoda Rule means to you and your power is that if you are seen as a source of support and encouragement you encourage your child four times as often as you criticize. Your child is having a tough time. School is a nightmare. Friendships are rocky. At least home can be a safe place. This means you need to be on the lookout for behaviors you can complement and reinforce. Understand that your positive comments are the most powerful reinforcer that you have. Believe it or not, your positive comments are more powerful than a trip to the toy store or an ice cream stand. Your child desperately wants to please you. The idea that you notice the positive things and encouraging suggesting him that he can please you. This is pure parenting gold. Use it wisely. Use it well.

Understand though, you can overdo it. At the ratio of 10 to 1, the performance starts to deteriorate. It appears too much positivity is not trusted or appreciated. And remember also that your positive comments need to be sincere. ADHD kids have powerful BS detectors so be authentic and sincere.

Setting limits is an act of love and caring.

Some of the most difficult situations I have seen in working with families involved teenagers who had never apparently heard the word no. By the time your child is a teenager it is too late to start setting limits and teaching the word "no". Start teaching "no" when your child is small. They need to understand that no matter how little and cute they are, there are still rules, there are still limits and mommy and daddy are there to enforce them. You have to be able to do this no matter how much they cry or pout or tantrum.

You're the big person and it's your responsibility to set limits. You have to understand that setting limits is an act of love and caring. Think of what happens if you let your toddler play in traffic. Part of your job setting limits to keep them safe, help them fit into society and help them develop a measure of self-discipline. I really feel sorry for kids that have no limits. They bounce along, taking all sorts of risks, doing all sorts of crazy things, secretly hoping that somebody will care enough to stop them. Sometimes parents do. Sometimes they don't.

Teach your child the valuable lesson of "no".

We've already talked about limiting criticism and the Lasoda Rule. I want to go a little further talking about the need to pick your spots. Sometimes it seems that parents just keep criticizing without really believing that anybody's hearing them. It seems more like they are ventilating for themselves than that they really expect any change in their child's behavior. Maybe they're trying to prove to their own parents, what good parents they are.

When you are considering discipline or any other corrective action (please God, not the dreaded lecture) you want to pick your spots carefully. If your child comes home from school after having the worst day ever, that is probably not the best time to get on him about making his bed. You want to pick a time when he is in a proper frame of mind to actually listen to what you have to say. You may also want to consider whether it's is important to say anything at all. If he's upset because he did poorly on the test that he argued with you about studying for then hallelujah! Natural consequences have taken over. You don't have to add to his upset with an "I told you so". This is the perfect time to commiserate with him and decide that he will study harder next time. Pick your spots.

Another area of concern in a strategic household is the ability to enforce what you say. Initially, when your child is young, you do not want to give orders that you can't enforce. Something on the order of "don't eat ice cream when you're with grandpa." This is not realistic. He's going to eat ice cream (grandpa is going to insist) and then he has a choice of either admitting it or lying to you. That's not a good way to train a child to be honest. It is best, especially initially for you to only have rules that you can enforce. This means behaviors you can actually see and hear. You have to start at this level and develop a pattern with your child in which he expects that if you give a rule, you will enforce it. Once you've established this pattern, you can occasionally give out rules that you won't be able to actually see or hear if he complies. Hopefully by that time, your child is well enough trained, sees the logic of your rules and will do his best to comply.

The last and most important thing once again is to maintain a long term perspective. You are adapting to having an ADHD child. You have a bigger job than the parents of neuro- typical children. I've raised both kinds of kids and let me tell you the neuro-typical kids are infinitely easier. With an ADHD child, you have to expect that you will spend some time in all those places you've been trying to avoid your whole life like the principal's office, the courtroom and maybe even, if you're really not lucky jail. Your job is to teach your ADHD child the skills he'll need to overcome, adapt and adjust to the pattern of deficits with which he was born. You need to remember it's not his fault. If you really need to blame somebody, blame an ancestor. Then get over it. You also have to deal with the fact that your ADHD child is, on average, three years behind his same age peers in terms of social development. This means you can pretty much give up the "but he should by now be able to..." He is at the level he is at and that's that. Accept it and deal with it.

Your job is to teach him time management skills, organizational skills, emotional control skills, basic learning skills and self acceptance. In a longitudinal study of ADHD children who became successful adults, the characteristics of the successful adults were: self-awareness, perseverance, proactivity, emotional stability, goal setting and being able to use support systems. This is your set of goals.

You want a child that is aware and accepting of himself. One who is able to persist even if the going gets tough, takes action, has learned to handle his emotions, can break a task down into smaller goals and achieve them. You want a child that recognizes when he needs help and has established a support system to assist him.

POINTS TO REMEMBER
- As a parent, your job is the manage the family, that is, keep it doing what it needs to do day to day
- You must maintain your power position in the family is to set the rules
- Your job is to set the rules for your family and enforce them

- Your child needs structure and routine. Provide it.
- Teach your child the word, "NO".
- Remember, setting limits is an act of love and caring.

Chapter 5: Leadership

Families that are strategic have parents who are leaders. They have a vision for the future of their children and family and they do the necessary to inspire and motivate their children to achieve that vision.

The vision is a broad-based one that emphasizes character and values rather than specific deeds and achievements. For instance, a leader would not insist that a child become an accountant but would try to ensure that the child becomes an adult with great integrity. The emphasis is on character rather than specific deeds. Typically, part of the vision is that the child will also become a leader and will work to improve their community and their society.

There are many ways to motivate and inspire children to achieve the vision. The first and most basic is to be a good role model. I've mentioned it before that what you do is many times more powerful than what you say. If you want children with integrity, you must display integrity yourself. You can't just order it. You must display it.

You must be aware of this fact and monitor your behavior accordingly. Children are very observant and they're really looking for someone to show them how they're supposed to live. The dad is supposed to show how a man, a father and a husband behave. The mom is supposed to show how a woman, wife and a mother behave. The two of them together show how a marriage and a family is supposed to work. They're supposed to show how adults work out problems even if they don't agree. They're supposed to show good negotiating skills and how to compromise without anger. It's a huge job and an important responsibility. Do not kid yourself that you can get away with doing stuff that doesn't meet the standard. The children may not confront you on it, but they will notice and they will learn.

I remember an example from my childhood of behavior that didn't meet the standard. A friend of my father's got drunk at a golf course and tried to drive home. He got into an accident and ran away from the scene. He hid the car in the garage and tried to straighten the bumper by hand causing a significant laceration on his hand. Eventually, the police came to his house and arrested him and led him away in handcuffs in front of his son who was about my age. My father's friend was only in jail over the weekend but he paid a significant fine, had a significant increase in his insurance and lost the respect of his son. His son began to act out, get in trouble and, by the way, began to drink abusively.

Another example from my own parenting involved an occasion when I was coaching my older son's baseball team. My younger son was either in the stands or working as a bat boy. MY team was not playing well and we getting outscored badly. The other team was not being particularly gentlemanly and were really giving us a lot of grief. Towards the end of the game we started to hit and made a comeback that made the score presentable, but we still lost. AT the end my team didn't want to shake hands with the other team. After a short discussion in which I did all the talking, my team, grudgingly went through the ritual of shaking hands with the other team. It took my youngest a long while before he understood that being a good sport does not depend on the behavior of the other team. Again, integrity is something I believe in absolutely. If you've got it no one can take it away.

Being a role model means that you're always aware of your position in the family hierarchy. Your behavior is important. Your keeping to your role is important. Don't lower yourself to arguing with your child. You may or may not win an argument, but you will have shown your child that he can make you lose your cool and possibly lose the argument. After that, it is hard to reassume the position of role model and leader. It can't be that important to you to win every argument. It can't necessitate that you actually argue with your child. Reason with them. Yes. Argue with them. No. You don't fuss and you don't throw temper tantrums. You show them the kind of respect and dignity that you expect in return.

You give directions clearly. You make sure that your child understands exactly what you expect. You use a calm voice; you speak clearly saying what you want and when you want it. You don't fuss. You don't yell or scream and you don't get physical.

I've seen families in which one or the other parent is always yelling. I wondered how this pattern became established. Then I realized that the parents had actually trained the child not to pay attention until one of the parents screamed or yelled. Then, the child knew that it was time to pay attention! So the child was actually waiting for the screaming to start before doing anything. I'm sure this wasn't what the parents had in mind; they just hadn't paid attention until the pattern was established.

A leader gives directions clearly and is aware of how he is giving the direction. There are no absent-minded corrections. If you are going to correct your child, you owe them the respect of paying attention to them and making sure your correction is accurate. Many parents give incredibly sloppy, imprecise directions and then are surprised when they don't get the response they expect. Be clear. Be concise. Pay attention to how your child responds. Make sure they understand what you want.

Another part of good leadership is to be under control. You're trying to direct and lead your family, specifically your child so that he becomes an adult that makes you proud. If you can't be calm, you might be better off waiting to deal with your child. If you had the world's worst day at work, this is probably not the time to take on why your son doesn't turn in his homework. You need to be in control. You need to be calm. Nobody is calm all the time and that's understandable but you need to be aware that you're a little frustrated or a little irritable and maybe now is not the best time to deal with your ADHD child. And never, and I mean never take out the frustrations of your day on your family!

One of the biggest lessons you can teach your child is how to delay gratification. Some experts think this is the single characteristic most responsible for success in life. It is also the characteristic that many parents fail to teach because it requires your child to face some frustration. The ability to delay gratification is what gets us through that chemistry class so we can graduate from high school. It is what gets us through all those prerequisite courses so we can graduate from college. And enables us to tolerate being poor while we build that business. It helps us take a position we don't like because it puts us in line to get a position we really want. This is one of those areas in which your child learns the most by observing you. Do you show that you can delay your own gratification for future good? In practically any behavior you are teaching your child, you have to show it first before you can teach it.

Once you are reasonably certain your child has seen you delay gratification, you can reasonably expect that it's time for you to teach him to delay gratification. You need to remember that to do this you are always comparing short-term to long-term. For example, you can do this now but if you wait you can do twice as much. If you really want a cookie, I'll give you one now but if you wait until after supper I'll give you three cookies. You're always giving choices and you must respect their choice. There are natural consequences to accepting less now rather than more later, namely you don't get the more later. A few times, your child will take the short term, but eventually he will learn that waiting a little bit to get the long-term is a more rewarding option. Not only is this a more valuable life lesson, but it spares you the nagging you get because they want what they want now!

That brings us once again to the long-term perspective. Always remember that you are in the process of training a child to be a responsible adult. Not to be the best bed maker in town or the adult with the cleanest bedroom. These are not the main things you are trying to train them to do. You want adults. You want people of integrity. You want people you can trust and be proud of. Remember that. Role model that. Try to teach that as much as you can, as often as you can.

You will be tempted to take the short term view. You will be tempted to argue. You will be tempted to yell and scream. Remember the difference between tactical and strategic. Tactical is short-term and focuses on winning the immediate battle. Strategic is long-term and focuses on winning the war. You can win a lot of battles and still lose the war. You can win every argument with your child and still having him living in your house at age 27. Wouldn't you rather have a responsible, reliable adult with integrity who brings his family to visit at Thanksgiving and Christmas? Think long-term. Think strategic.

For more tips on developing leadership parenting skills visit my blog at www.AHDHStrategicParenting.com.

POINTS TO REMEMBER
- Leadership means you are taking your family from where they are on a transformative journey to where they can be—your child as a responsible adult.
- You, as a parent, are a leader and a role model
- Your job is display those character traits you want in your child
- Your behavior is that of a leader, maintaining emotional control.

76

- You give directions clearly and calmly.
- You give directions mindfully, that is, you are paying attention to your child.
- You do all in your power to inspire and motivate your child.

Chapter 6: Mentoring I

Another big job associated with raising an ADHD child is mentoring. Mentoring is just a fancy word for teaching. Ideally, teaching your child what he needs to be successful in the world. With ADHD children the demands are a little more specific and a little more urgent. We have mentioned before many areas of difficulty that ADHD children have. They have problems with organization. They have poor working memory. They tend to be easily overwhelmed by academic requirements. They have no time sense. They procrastinate. They are emotionally fragile and impulsive. They tend to be easily discouraged and to give up.

These difficulties are all caused by their ADHD. It is the result of a neurologic condition. You, as the parent have the job of teaching them how to deal with these difficulties. Fortunately, there is a considerable amount of information in my field, good old psychology that can help you in these situations.

You'll want to teach your child how to set goals, how to get organized, how to control his or her emotions, how to persevere, sometimes called resilience. As previously mentioned there are many good workbooks and courses that will teach you how to teach your child. I'll briefly summarize the main components for some of the basic ones.

ORGANIZATION

One of the major areas of difficulty is how to get organized. We're talking about organization in the sense of – how do I get that class project done? An ADHDer will tend to look at the project as a huge complicated difficult task that will require hours and hours of time. He will then start to feel overwhelmed and want to give up.

1. Your first job is to teach him that any project is composed of many small tasks that don't take very much time.
2. Then you teach him to identify and list those tasks.
3. Then you teach him to organize them so that they get done in a reasonable order. You want to get your child to see that some steps come before others.
4. Then help them estimate how long it will take to accomplish each task.
5. Then you calculate how much time you need to do every day or every week to get the project done on time.
6. Then you decide on a time to do it. Then you set your trusty timer for the appropriate length of time and get started.

You have now taught your ADHD child a system for getting projects done. When your ADHD child understands there is a structure and the system for completing big tasks, they will be able to approach new tasks with less panic. Logic and organization are always the enemies of anxiety, panic and procrastination.

TIME MANAGEMENT

Time management is closely linked to organization. Again, the approach is to develop a system that works to keep track of all the things that need to be done every day. The problem with most time management systems is that they tend to be designed for linear logical types who are mildly compulsive. These are the people who outline everything and file everything in alphabetical order. Now these are very good systems for people who will actually use them. I must confess that I am most comfortable with this kind of system. Unfortunately, many if not most ADHDers view these systems as a form of punishment. They get bored and they quit using them.

Many, if not most ADHDers are visual-spatial organizers. They actually have to see stuff to even know it's there. Their filing system tends to be horizontal. That is, every flat space is covered with different stacks of paper. It seems as though ADHDers have to actually see things to remember to work with them. Using clear containers with appropriate labels is vital to these people.

Another vital consideration is the use of color in addition to words and numbers and letters. For instance, color coding of different courses in school may involve an appropriately colored label on a clear storage bin of class materials or a color-coded file folder. Even if the use of color doesn't make sense to you, you should give it a try. You might be surprised and how easy it is for your child to find information when you have color-coded it.

A more modern concern in the 21st century world is whether to use old-fashioned strategies involving writing things down, organizing papers in folders and so on or to use technology. This will depend on your child's comfort level and expertise in using technology. Probably, most children are considerably more comfortable with technology than their parents. The point is, if they'll use it, then it will be incredibly effective in improving their organization and time management skills. If they won't use it because it's clunky, it's the wrong color, it's boring or whatever, it doesn't really matter if you like the system. If your child doesn't, it won't get used and it's worthless.

I'm kind of old school. I have a cell phone, a tablet and several laptops but I still prefer an old-fashioned paper and pen pocket calendar. I use the system called Daytimer, mostly because I've been using it for 30 years and am comfortable with it. I like the idea of just being able to write things down without having to open a mobile device, insert my password and go to the appropriate app. With the Daytimer, I just open it up and start writing.

I even use their system of writing down what I need to accomplish in a given day and then prioritizing it so I know which thing to do first. It's a real simple system, I don't have to think about it much and it gives me enough organization/ time management help to be reasonably efficient.

Your ADHD child is probably not going to be interested in an old-fashioned paper tracking system like mine but, if they are, one of the advantages is that there are numerous covers in various styles or colors for the calendars and they can select one from the catalog or store that they like. It can be a fun thing to do and it increases your child's feeling of ownership which increases his desire to make the system work.

If they are more into the technology solutions (and why wouldn't they be?), just make sure that they have actually mastered whatever app in whatever system they'll be using.

The way you introduce time management/organization to your child will make all the difference. Do not, under any circumstances, just decide what they need and order them to use it. Make it a collaborative effort. Talk about their difficulties with time management and then go over the options. See what piques their interest and follow that. You will find that this makes the whole procedure much easier. You may even find that they and you enjoyed the process.

After you have made the decision about how to organize and manage time, you help with implementation. You make sure they know what they need to do. You check with them periodically to see if they are having any problems. You want to continually impress on them the importance of managing time and being organized. You also want to enforce the idea that it is a relatively simple, logical procedure and it makes life easier.

Part of organization and time management involves actually measuring time. For some children and some ages you can get away with the a guesstimate of duration such as "about 30 minutes". Not so for your ADHD child. Remember that

ADHD children have very poor time sense, that is, they're not very good at estimating the passage of time. Therefore, they need a timer. If they're into technology, they can use the timer on their electronic organizing device or phone. If they are less into technology, a kitchen timer, perhaps even the Pomodoro (tomato) timer recommended earlier in this book may work. Actually, the Pomodoro timer may be the best for both groups because it is interesting and unusual and slightly amusing. You want as much of this new learning to be entertaining and fun as is possible. Having a bright red tomato timer on your desk is all the above!

EMOTIONAL CONTROL

One of the major areas that cause difficulties for ADHDers is the control of emotions. ADHDers tend to be more emotional than those without the condition. They tend to go off on emotional tangents. They get extremely angry, extremely frustrated, extremely sad, extremely tearful or extremely just about any other emotion. The bad news is, they don't think they can control their emotions. The good news is they can be taught to control their emotions.

First, you have to make sure that you, as the parent, believe that we are in control of our emotions. If you don't believe that then you have some problems with this section. Also, you're not alone. As a psychologist, I am frequently amazed that people believe more strongly that they can lose 50 pounds in the next month than believe that they have control over their emotions!

One of the blessings of late 20th century psychology has been the growth of cognitive therapy. This therapeutic approach is variously attributed to Aaron T Beck, Albert Ellis and/or Donald Michenbaum. The basic premise is that emotions are under our control, specifically by the way we think about things. We are not the victim of unconscious impulses, conflicts or trauma. Our emotions are the product of how we think. We are trained in how we think by our parents and caregivers. Unfortunately, most of us never really make the connection that we have a choice about our emotional responses. We tend to think that they just happened without our having any control at all. Fortunately, nothing could be further from the truth.

To help your child control his emotions, you have to first present the notion that they have control and that their emotions are the results of the way they are thinking about a given situation. Fortunately, with an ADHD child, it is usually pretty obvious what they are thinking about a specific situation because they're screaming it!

The next step is for you to capture what they're saying. This may be best done with your cell phone. Simply record their conversation. Do not challenge them while they're upset. This would lead to even more problems. But, after they calm down, get them alone and introduced the idea that thinking causes emotions. Explain that thoughts that cause extreme emotions are exaggerated and that this exaggeration is what causes us to be so upset. Then play the recording and see if your child can see the exaggerations in what he is screaming. They may even have fun doing it.

The central idea is not that we are not supposed to have emotions but that the emotions we should have are relatively mild. If we are having really strong negative emotions, it's because our thoughts are exaggerated and even irrational. So what the parent is essentially doing is training the child to be logical and to see the illogic in some of his thinking. We all have irrational, exaggeratedly negative thoughts. Examples include: he always... Or they always... Or nothing good ever happens to me or I can tell this is going to be a terrible day.

These are all exaggeratedly negative thoughts that if examined them closely, are irrational. You can't really say he always does anything because nobody always does something. And no one always has bad things happen to them with no good things ever happening. And no day is ever completely good or completely bad.

So what you want your child to say is something more logical and less exaggerated. Instead of "nothing good ever happens to me." Try "I've had some bad things happen to me but I've also had some good things happen. I'll try to pay as much attention to the good things as the bad things."

You, as the parent are teaching your child to speak more realistically which leads to viewing the world more realistically which leads to thinking more realistically. Eventually you are hoping that they will be able to do this on their own. This by itself increases their emotional control. Understand, it is not going to happen instantly. It will take some time, some patience and some effort.

One way to add structure to this process is to use a three column technique. Divide a piece of paper into three columns. One column describes the situation, the emotion and how bad it was a scale of 1 to 10. The next column captures what the irrational, exaggerated thoughts were. The third column is the more logical evaluation of the situation which should lead to reduced emotion.

It is vitally important to teach your child that emotions don't just happen. Teach them that they have control over their emotions. Many people think that events cause emotions. If this were true we would all have the same emotion in the same situation. Consider the most frequent venue for irrational emotions and behavior – driving your car. Everybody's in the same situation so everybody should probably have the same emotions. But, if you look you'll see some drivers look absolutely terrified, with a white knuckle grip on the steering wheel and an expression of extreme fear. You'll see some other people are just chilling, talking on their cell phones, looking around, not paying attention at all to their driving. You will also see some drivers who are angry, mad even, shaking their fists, screaming at other drivers with the veins bulging in their foreheads.

Same situation, different emotions. Why is that? Because each person has a different set of irrational thoughts about the situation. The fearful driver is focusing on thoughts about being involved in a catastrophic accident and thinks the cure for that is to drive extremely carefully. The driver that's chilling has convinced himself that driving is a time to catch up on text messages and that there's absolutely no danger. The angry driver has convinced himself that no one should be in his way. That it's his road and he should be able to go as fast as he wants to without any hindrance. Obviously none of these thoughts are logical, rational or correct. They do illustrate the point that the way we think causes our emotional reaction. Probably the most extreme example of this is illustrated by Victor Frankel, a psychiatrist who was in a Nazi concentration camp during World War II. The conditions were horrible. Prisoners were underfed and basically worked to death. Even in this situation, Frankel observed that some of the prisoners were able to maintain a more positive mindset than the others. The prisoners with a positive mindset tended to survive and were eventually rescued by the Allies. The ones who lost hope tended to sicken and die. This is further proof that events don't cause emotions. The view we take of those events is what causes our emotions.

If you can teach your child this skill, he will have made the first step towards being resilient which is a fancy word for stress proof. If your child knows that the way he thinks about things ultimately determines the way he feels, then he will learn that he is ultimately in control. This makes it much easier for your child to tolerate the negative things that inevitably happen to a child with ADHD.

Your child will learn to never give up. He will learn to take adversity. He will learn to stay level emotionally and also learn to keep trying. Another side benefit they will learn and you should reinforce is that *effort* is the most important attribute to personal success.

You should never ever let your child think that success is a result of anything more than hard work and discipline. If you let them start thinking that success is the result of some genetic trait or natural attribute, you are going to have great difficulty getting them to put in the extra effort they're going to need to succeed against neuro-typical kids who don't have ADHD.

You need to examine your own beliefs about success and what causes it. Most of the people reading this book are from America, the home of self-made men and women, yet we continuously attribute success to some inherited trait like intelligence. Intelligence is mostly the result of training, repetition and effort.

Did you know that in Japan they don't even have the concept of IQ? They believe that if you did better on a test than somebody else, it's because you worked harder and studied more. I am continually meeting children who have decided that they are not very smart, that they don't have the right genes and therefore it's okay for them to give up on education.

This is a catastrophe and it causes lifelong difficulties. The other day, I was testing a 70-year-old man who had decided (and no doubt been told) that he wasn't very smart and would never succeed in school. As a result, he majored in industrial arts in high school (this was back in the days when it was possible to do this). He took an industrial job and worked hard his entire life. When I tested him, every time we had to do something related to language he came very close to a panic attack. Yet when I tested him, he had above average IQ! I don't mean that everybody has to go to college to be happy with life but clearly this gentleman was severely traumatized by his educational experiences and had never truly recovered. I firmly believe that everyone should be encouraged to achieve as much as they can in whatever way they can.

Hopefully, you would want better for your child than what this gentleman experienced. Teaching them that they are in control of their emotions and that they should never give up and that effort is the key to success are the ways to keep this from happening. Keep trying, learn from mistakes errors and failures and use those lessons to improve performance. Learning this and doing this all starts in childhood and it is vital for you to teach your child that effort, trying, doing is the key to being successful.

Do you know one of the biggest mistakes parents make with a child that gets good grades? They praise the child for being intelligent not for the amount of effort they put into their academics. The problem is, praising intelligence is a little like praising blue eyes. You are praising an attribute that the child doesn't control. Therefore when they get into a situation in which the material is harder and success is more difficult, they are likely to give up, figuring they're not intelligent enough to do well in this environment.

You see it all the time, particularly in college. A group of new freshmen arrive on campus and they're all going to be doctors, lawyers and nuclear physicists. After one semester, they're all majoring in education or general studies or they've dropped out of school and enlisted in the military. I don't mean that there's anything wrong with either of these two academic areas or joining the military, but it's a result of giving up. If, instead of being praised for intelligence, they were praised for the effort they put in or the hours they spent reading, they would know that a tougher challenge necessitates a tougher response.

In order to succeed, you've got to put more effort into studying, and figure out a better or more efficient approach. It doesn't matter if your eyes are blue or your high school GP was 4.0, what matters is how you rise to the challenge. This is probably the most important thing you need to teach your child.

All children make mistakes. ADHD children probably make more mistakes than most. You can spend all your time berating them for making mistakes or you can teach them to learn from mistakes. This is true even if, to you, it is blatantly obvious that your child should not have done what they did. No, you shouldn't attach a waterski tow rope to your friends bicycle and have him tow you on your skateboard. No, you shouldn't jump off the garage roof into a pile of leaves. (Guess who's son did both of these?) Also, you shouldn't call a teacher a freaking liar because she got to the scene of the crime late and didn't see what precipitated your response. In spite of the nobility of your defending the Down Syndrome kid against the bullies, you got punished. They didn't. (Yep, mine again)

As a parent you have to do some "lessons-learned" work. For example, you can ask your child — instead of calling the teacher a freaking liar, what could you have said that would've explained the situation a little better? Maybe, before you jump off the roof you should check how deep the leaf pile is. Or maybe you could take some para course lessons and learn how to land and roll and avoid hurting yourself.

Also, you need to remember that there is no such thing as one trial learning with an ADHD child. With some kids, they do something, there's a bad outcome or they get hurt and they will not want to do it again. Not so much with ADHD kids. They have a marvelous ability to forget what happened before and to not recognize that the new situation is startlingly similar to the old situation! Therefore, you have to keep repeating the same "what did you learn from this?" Fortunately, eventually it kicks in and they learn to anticipate consequences themselves.

USING SUPPORT

One of the other skills it's vital to teach an ADHD child is how to use support systems and eventually how to build their own support system. Having and using support systems is one of the characteristics of successful adults with ADHD. The stereotype is the creative but disorganized executive with an extremely organized administrative assistant who keeps him organized. The current model is more likely to be the creative but disorganized entrepreneur whose business would go into bankruptcy if not for his organized partner.

The parents, of course, are or should be the ADHD child's first support system. However, it doesn't hurt to include other people in the mix. Sports coaches, martial arts instructors, teachers, psychologists, youth ministers can all have a role to play. Also, classmates can be helpful and encouraging. All of these people in all of these different roles can either be helpful or extremely hurtful. You, as the parent need to monitor your child's interactions with these people.

One of the significant components of many support systems is that it is mutually beneficial. Betty shares her notes with your child and your child helps her develop creative ideas for her school project. It is important that your child learn that he should give something back to the relationship.

The biggest awareness that you're trying to develop is your child's awareness of when his ADHD is likely to cause difficulties. For instance, does your child have difficulties paying attention and taking notes? Does your child have difficulties remembering the necessary books to do homework? Your child needs to learn that there are ways to deal with these situations. Do you get the teacher involved and ask her to provide notes? Is there somebody in the class it takes exceptionally good notes and would be willing to share in return for something your child can offer? You want your child to realize when his ADHD is going to cause difficulties and develop strategies to deal with those situations. Frequently the strategy will involve another person. You want your child to become familiar with how support systems work at an early age.

As he gets older, your child will likely make more frequent use of support systems. He will have to be comfortable asking for help. They will also have to be aware of the other person's needs and be able to offer something in return for their assistance. This brings up how using support systems help your child learn to negotiate. It is an important skill, particularly as one gets older to learn to negotiate. It is a skill to start introducing when your child is in middle school. Learning to negotiate is a way for your child to learn how the adult world operates. He will learn that he has to give some to get some.

This is a vital skill to teach your child before he becomes a teenager. I have had numerous families in my office that neglected this step with the result that their child was still using the strategies of a two-year-old to get his way and totally not understand that you have to give something back to get what you want. It's quite an experience to watch a near six-foot tall 14-year-old boy stamp his feet and holler like a two-year-old. It is definitely unattractive and represents a skill deficit that can cause that difficulties, probably for the rest of his life.

This child never learned to appropriately negotiate. He did not recognize the power situation in his own home or at school and frequently, not even with his friends. To negotiate, you have to be aware of what your power situation is. Have you been on your best behavior for the last two weeks? Was your report card good last week? Have you been doing all your chores? If you have all these things going for you, you have some power based on the goodwill you've generated with your parents. This would be a good time to ask for permission to do something extra.

As the child you also have to understand the power position of the person with whom you are negotiating. When it's your parents, one of the things you have to understand, like it or not, is that they are responsible for you. There are laws that they must obey regarding their care and treatment of you and your siblings. They are required to do all they can to keep you safe, keep you healthy and get you educated. Anybody else with whom you negotiate will also have certain circumstances that limit their power. When you are negotiating, you have to keep both of these things in mind. You have to be aware of the effect your request has on their situation. If you don't go to school, sure, you get into trouble. But, your parents also get into trouble.

In the part of tidewater Virginia where I live, we had a recent situation in which some parents decided that it would be better to let their teenagers drink at home rather than around some bonfire in the woods. Guess what? The police didn't agree. Both parents were arrested, jailed, had to go to court, had to go back to jail, plus pay a healthy fine. This represents what should have been a non-negotiable situation.

Analyzing the power aspects of different relationships along with how to gain influence and power in an ethical way are part of what should be taught to your child to help them negotiate. Your child needs to know that they first analyze the situation to better understand how the request affects the other person. Then, they calmly present their request, hopefully being able to tell their parents what the benefits are for everyone. Then being able to answer parental objections calmly and reasonably.

This is negotiation. There is no room for anger, temper tantrums, yelling and screaming and certainly no stamping feet or destroying property. This is a skill that should be formally taught to your ADHD child. As soon as you can, teach your child to negotiate and become aware of situations in which his ADHD causes him difficulties. Teach him solutions to these problems and teach him how to establish a support network to help him cope with difficult situations.

As an adult, your child will have to be comfortable asking for assistance. Sometimes, people have difficulties asking for help. They think it indicates that they are weak or not very bright. The thing they need to remember is that everybody needs help sometimes. No successful person – great scientist, great musician, great businessman, great actor or great entrepreneur – ever did it all by themselves. You need to teach your child how to ask for help and how to offer something in return. This will allow them to develop and grow a support system that enables them to be successful.

POINTS TO REMEMBER

- Your primary job as a parent has always been to be a mentor, a teacher to your child.
- Fortunately the areas that an ADHD child has difficulties in can be trained.
- You must train your child in basic organization skills, how break a task into smaller parts and complete them in a logical order.
- Time management is a trainable ability, teach your ADHD child how to improve his awareness of and use of time.
- Teach your child emotional regulation techniques. It is a learnable that will help him throughout his life.
- Teach your child to develop and use a support system. He must start with being aware of when and in what situations, his ADHD will get in the way.
- Teach your child how to negotiate. It's a valuable skill throughout life and involves maintaining emotional control and being aware of the other person's needs and motivations.

Chapter 7: Mentoring II

MEDITATION/RELAXATION/TRAINING

Continuing with the theme of mentoring your ADHD child by providing them with skills training in areas of deficit caused by their ADHD, we now proceed to meditation/relaxation training. Meditation and/or relaxation training have in recent years been shown to be extremely helpful for ADHD children. In no way does it cure ADHD but it does improve your child's life. There are some indications that it actually causes positive changes in the brain that may improve attention and concentration. It is definitely helpful in reducing emotional intensity and outbursts. Actually, it is a helpful skill for all of us, not just ADHD kids.

I'm just going to call it meditation from now on but understand that I'm basically including all the methods of reducing tension and stress. Meditation is a group of techniques that allows people to reduce tension and stress and increase focus. Every culture and every religion has a group of techniques that accomplish these goals.

There are four characteristics to all meditation techniques:
   1. A comfortable position

2. Minimal environmental distractions
3. A mental focus point
4. A passive set of mind

These characteristics are mostly obvious. You want to be able to sit comfortably. You don't want a lot of noise in the environment around you. You need something to pay attention to. You need to accept what happens without trying to force it (that's the passive part).

The mental focus can be any of a number of things. The idea is that you're paying attention to your focus rather than to all the thoughts that are causing you discomfort. The mental focus tends to be of two major types – physiological or imaginal. Physiological foci include paying attention to one's breath, one's muscle tension, one's sensory information. Imaginal foci tend to involve various visualization techniques involving developing a peaceful scene in your mind using all of your senses.

In general the physiological foci tend to involve a lot of repetition such as paying attention to your breath and counting or saying a short phrase or word with each exhalation. These are the easiest techniques to understand but they require the most discipline to sustain. The imaginal foci are relatively easier to sustain because the visualization is more likely to hold attention. Also, ADHD children tend, on average, to be more visual and kinesthetic than just verbal.

Remember, meditation/relaxation training are skills. It is necessary to practice and master them. They are not like an aspirin. You have to have done the necessary practice and training before you can expect to get significant results.

VISUALIZATION

Here is a script for a visualization that I frequently use:

Settle down in your chair. Shift your weight a little and get comfortable. Then let your eyes close and just listen to the sound of my voice. First just let a number drift in your mind that represents how much tension you feel. We'll use a 10 point scale with one being almost no tension and 10 being as much tension as you can imagine. Once you've got that number in mind, we will continue on.

I'm going to describe a beach scene that I enjoy. I'm going to provide some details, but don't worry if you imagine something a little different. Feel free to change the images to suit yourself. After all, this is supposed to be relaxing.

Imagine yourself walking along the beach. It's a beautiful sunny day. The sky is blue with just a few white puffy clouds. The sun is bright and warm and comfortable overhead. You can feel the heat of the sun on the top of your head on your shoulders and a little bit less on your back and neck.

You're walking along the sand, which is warm under your feet but not too hot. You hear the sound of the waves as they break and come to the shore and then recede back out to deeper water. And then they come back again over... And over... And over.

Pleasant comfortable sound of the waves breaking on the shore, the sun overhead warming your head and neck and shoulders. Watching the waves break. Watching the sun make patterns on the water. Looking at the sun in the sky and the clouds.

There are some boats out on the water. At least one of them is a sailboat and I can't quite make out the color of the sail but I'm sure you can. I can't tell if it's all one color, maybe white or maybe it's a bunch of colors in some design pattern. I can't really tell but perhaps you can.

I know the wind where you are is gentle, but maybe it's stronger further from shore. Again I'm not sure but maybe you can tell.

There are also some seabirds, some gulls and some other birds are flying around, busily looking for food. You can hear them calling as they fly around. You can also smell the salty air.

The warm sun overhead, the waves lapping at the shore, the smell of the salty air, the sounds of the birds.

You start walking down the beach. It's not very crowded today. There are not a lot of people. You enjoy the sensation of walking along feeling the sun on your body and the movement of your muscles and the feeling of your feet in the soft warm sand.

You stop and look around and then you sit down in the sand, feeling the warmth of the sun on your upper body and the warmth of the sand below you.

You lie down in the sand and close your eyes and just enjoy the warmth of the sun above you and the warmth of the sand below you. The sound of the waves as they break along the shore. The sound of the seabirds calling to one another. The feeling of the breeze blowing across your body, the smell of the salty air, the distant sounds of people's voices and you can even hear the breeze as it blows across the sand.

You settle down into the sand feeling the warmth of the sand and noticing how it's allowing your muscles to relax. Your muscles relax all the way from the top your head to the soles of your feet. Top of your head down the back of your head and neck, down your shoulders, your back and legs all the way down to your feet. Your muscles giving up tension, lengthening becoming more comfortable and at ease.

Feeling extremely calm and peaceful. You let yourself stay in this position. Feeling the warmth of the sun, the warmth of the sand, the smell of the sea, the sound of the waves, the sound of the seabirds, the breeze against your skin.

Relax, comfortable, at peace and at ease.

You've decided that you like this place and you're comfortable here and you can use this place as your special place and come back to it whenever you feel like you'd like to slow down and relax and get more comfortable.

I'm going to let you enjoy your time here for as long as you'd like.

When you feel like it, just open your eyes, adjust to this room, the place from which you started. Before you do anything else think back to the 1 to 10 stress scale and let a new number float into your mind indicating your current level of stress. Probably it is a good bit lower. And, when you feel like it go ahead and stand up feeling relaxed and refreshed calm and confident.

That's right, that's right.

Potentially, you could use the script with your ADHD child. You have to remember a couple of things. One, your voice quality is almost as important as what you say. Your voice needs to sound relaxed and comfortable. Two, read slowly and comfortably. Don't rush and don't worry if you misread something and certainly don't make a big deal out of it. This needs to be a relaxing experience for everybody. You may just want to record this script and play it back so that both you and your child can have a relaxing experience.

PROGRESSIVE MUSCLE RELAXATION

Progressive muscle relaxation is based on the notion developed by an Austrian physiologist named Jacobson who observed that a tense muscle actually relaxed after the tension was increased. The basic theory is, you go through the major muscle groups in the body, tensing each one and letting the tension out quickly. This helps reduce stress and tension in the mind and the body. Also because it is relatively active, it is easier to do and get good results even with someone who has no experience in meditation or relaxation training. For me, it is my last resort technique when my mind is just tied up over something and nothing else works.

Here is the progressive muscle relaxation script:

First, settle comfortably in your chair. Ideally it is an armchair but it is possible to get good results with any kind of chair. Close your eyes and let your mind wander. Now, using a scale from 1 to 10 where one indicates virtually no tension and 10 represents the most tension you can imagine, let a number representing your current level of tension flash in your mind and remember it.

We're going to go through progressive muscle relaxation, which involves tensing the different muscle groups. You'll be told where to start and what to do. When you tense a muscle, remember to tense it to about 85% of your full effort. Don't ever squeeze so hard that you hurt yourself.

We're going to begin with a lower body.
1. Starting with your calves, we're going to tense those muscles by pointing the toes away from the body. Point. Point. Point. Point. Now, let go let go of the tension in your muscles. Feel the difference between the muscles when they were tense and tight and now that they're warm and relaxed and comfortable.
2. Now, point your toes toward your knees. Again, hold that tension for 3 to 5 seconds and then let go. And again after letting go notice the difference in the muscles between being cold and tense and tight and being warm and loose and relaxed.
3. (Now I'll just go through the different muscle groups and what the tension movement is. Every time you tense hold it for 3 to 5 seconds and then suddenly release the tension and focus on the muscle and the difference you feel now that it's relaxed.)
4. Thighs. Tense these by raising your legs straight out and holding the tension for 3 to 5 seconds.

5. Gluteus maximus (buttocks) – this is an area that has a lot of tension because in modern life, we spend a lot of time sitting on them. Increase the tension by squeezing your cheeks together (you will undoubtedly get some giggles from your ADHD child here!) Hold the tension, release, focus.

6. Abdomen – tense the abdominal muscles by inhaling and then, as you exhale pull your stomach in and up and hold it. Hold the tension, release, focus.

7. Chest – tense these muscles by first inhaling and then squeeze down on the breath, holding it, while assuming the Superman pose like you're showing off your muscles. Hold the tension, release, focus.

8. Back – you get the long muscles in your back by arching against your chair so that the only part of your back touching is the shoulder area. Hold the tension, release, focus. This one shouldn't be an issue for an ADHD child, but a parent with back problems should be very careful about too much tension in this position. Be a little more cautious than on other positions.

9. Forearms –palmar surface – you tense this area by making fists and squeezing. Again, hold attention, release, focus.

10. Forearms – dorsal surface – tense this area by first putting your arms on the armrest, palms down. Now raise your fingers towards the sky as far as you can go. Hold the tension, release, focus.

11. Biceps – tense this area by again making fists and raise your fists toward your shoulder, tightening the bicep muscle. Hold the tension, release, focus.

12. Back of the arms – tense this area by pushing your elbows against the back of your chair. Hold the tension, release, focus.
13. Shoulders – tense this area by raising your shoulders in an exaggerated shrug as if your shoulders could cover your ears. Hold the tension, release, focus.
14. Neck – tense the front of the neck by putting your chin to your chest and pushing. Hold the attention, release, focus.
15. Neck – dorsal – tense the back your neck by putting your head against the back of the chair or the wall and pushing. Hold the tension, release, focus.
16. Face – forehead – tense this area by raising your eyebrows as high as you can. Hold the attention, release, focus.
17. Face – eyes – tense this area by closing your eyes and squeezing them tightly shut. Hold the tension, release, focus.
18. Face – mouth – you tense this area, which stores a surprising amount of tension, by opening your mouth as wide as you can and sticking your tongue out. The sticking your tongue out will doubtless cause giggles and can be eliminated if necessary. Hold the tension, release, focus.
19. Face – jaw – be very careful tensing this area. The masseters (the small walnut sized muscles that close the jaw) are very powerful and can break fillings and teeth. Again, be very careful. You tense this area by setting your upper teeth down on your lower teeth and squeezing carefully. Hold the tension, release, focus.

The last phase of this exercise is to very quickly review all of the muscle groups that you've gone through. Just let your mind go over your body. If you find areas where there is still tension just do another of the exercises to tense and loosen that area. The last thing is to again find your stress scale, 1 to 10, and find the number for your current level of stress. Remember, 1 means little or no tension, 10 means the most tension you can imagine.

BREATHING FOCUS MEDITATION

Breathing focus meditation is the simplest to explain and probably the hardest to do because it's so simple. People tend to get bored and distracted. This can be even more of an issue for your ADHD child. Nonetheless, if they get to the point where they can actually do this for 20 minutes, they have shown an admirable amount of effort which should be praised.

Because breathing focus meditation is relatively unstructured, or its over-structured depending on your point of view, I'm not going to provide a full script. The basic procedure is to sit quietly, focus on your breathing knowing that your attention will wander periodically. When it does, gently bring your focus back to your breathing. At first, your mind will be wandering off fairly often. However, as you become more accustomed to meditation, you will be able to maintain focus for longer and longer periods of time.

The simplest form of breathing focus meditation is to purely focus on the breath. Feel it come in, feel it stop, feel it go out, feel it stop again, over and over and over.

The second simplest form was developed by Dr. Herbert Spencer and involves merely saying "one" with each exhalation. This approach was developed based on his studies of transcendental meditation and his desire to simplify and westernize it.

The next simplest form is to repeat either a word or a short phrase that is meaningful to you. This can be a Sanskrit word, a religious thought (God is love, etc.), a general spiritual thought (peace and love, love and understanding, etc.) or a helpful reminder (Let Go, Release, Breathe Freely, etc.)

So, the basic session involves sitting quietly, clearing your mind, establishing what your tension/stress level is on a 1 to 10 scale and then focusing on your breathing and with each exhalation saying to yourself whatever it is you've decided will be helpful. Personally, I would pick something like "Let Go" or "Release" to start. These are just nice neutral terms that don't cause people to wander off into all sorts of distracting thoughts.

Initially, attempt to get five minutes of meditating done. Then gradually increase two minutes at a time until you are able to do 20 minutes comfortably. Since you want to be able to keep your eyes closed and your focus inward, I would recommend using the timer on your watch or phone or any other time or you have that doesn't make noise while it is timing. Preferably, you want one that has a gentle alarm so that you come out of your meditative state calm and focused not startled and disgruntled. After you finish, again find yourself on your 1 to 10 tension/stress scale.

GENERAL INSTRUCTIONS

This set of instructions can help you and your child share the experience of meditating. As the parent, you have more responsibility for both becoming familiar with the scripts and the procedures and monitoring your child's reactions.

Some parents choose to read the scripts and observe. Some parents record the scripts and play them so that both the parent and the child can devote more attention to the meditative experience. Either way, remember, this is a valuable skill that will help both of you. It will help your child develop better emotional control and focus. It will help you develop more calm and less frustration.

Just in case, you have some objections to meditation on religious grounds, just remember that there is a powerful tradition of meditative prayer in the Christian religion and indeed, in every other religion or spiritual practice in the world. If your objections to meditation are that it is some kind of "woo woo" New Age kind of stuff, understand that many professional athletes and professional sports teams, including football players, meditate to improve their performances. If it's manly enough for some 300 pound defensive lineman than it's probably manly enough for you and I.

In my experience, the mothers don't have as much resistance to meditation as the fathers. Perhaps it's the result of all the yoga classes at all the gyms and exercise centers. Perhaps it's just that women are more comfortable experimenting with new things. Whatever the reason, I just haven't come across any resistance from the mothers to trying meditation.

I highly recommend you give meditation a try. Initially I'd start with your ADHD child, but eventually I would try to include the entire family. You will likely be amazed at how much calmer and quieter and more peaceful your home life can become if everyone in the family meditates 15 to 20 minutes a day.

The psychological benefits have been thoroughly researched and proven. There are numerous reports of decreased anxiety, decreased tension, decreased stress, decreased pain, improved alertness, improved attention, improved energy and improve general attitude as a result of meditation.

Physically, there is considerable research supporting the notion of reduced pain secondary to meditation. John Kabat-Zinn, psychologist at Massachusetts General Hospital, long ago instituted meditation as a key component in his pain management program. There also confirmed reports of reduced headaches, reduced flareups of irritable bowel syndrome, decreased asthma attacks, better responses to medication secondary to meditation. There are also reports of increased performance in athletes, musicians and other performance artists.

As I said previously, meditation cannot only improve your ADHD child's focus and emotional control it can also help the rest of the family achieve better focus and emotional control and make home life more comfortable for all.

Additional techniques for gaining more focus can be found at my website www.ADHDStrategicParenting.com.

POINTS TO REMEMBER

- Meditation is a valuable skill particularly for an ADHD child. It helps with control of emotions and actually helps improve control of attention.
- Meditation is a learned skill that must be practiced regularly to obtain good results.
- Meditation can be taught by the parents to an ADHD child.
- Meditation can be useful to the entire family.
- The parent should go through one of the provided scripts alone until comfortable with the procedure.
- Presenting meditation to the child can be done by reading the script or by recording it ahead of time and replaying it.
- The most important component is not so much what you say but how you say it. Use a calm, unhurried voice and breathe slowly and easily.

CONCLUSION

We come to the conclusion of this attempt to provide some clarification and tools for dealing with an ADHD child. My hope is that parents of ADHD children that read this book will be better prepared to raise them to become responsible adults...and have less fear and chaos along the way. That is the entire focus of this book and the characteristic that separates strategic parenting from more tactical approaches.

This is the first book in a planned series of books about ADHD children and the unique parenting concerns associated with raising them. The next book is about being a powerful parent to your ADHD child. I have over my years as a therapist seen countless examples of how couples, well-meaning and frequently well-educated, make themselves powerless in dealing with their children. This has significant consequences for the family. It is difficult to have a happy organized life if the children are in charge at home.

One of the things that you need to prepare yourself for as your child matures and moves out into the world is that it's not over. Even if you have taught your son or daughter all the skills we describe, if you have managed your household and yourself accordingly and done a really outstanding job in all things, you still have an ADHD child who is now an ADHD adult. This means that, on average, your young adult is three years behind his peers in terms of emotional maturity. He's still going to be impulsive. He's still going to take greater the normal risks. He's still going to get bored and frustrated with routine. He is still going to crave excitement.

An ADHD adult is not someone who thinks inside the box. ADHDers are outside the box thinkers who value freedom and independence over everything. They have little tolerance or patience for boring, repetitive tasks. They do not fit into the cubicle workspace. Their idea of hell is to sit in a cubicle all day moving papers from their inbox to their outbox.

As a parent, you may have different goals for your child than he has for himself. Most parents want their children to have nice secure jobs, to meet and marry a nice person that they can bring home to mom and to eventually have a couple of children that grandma and grandpa can spoil. ADHDers are not necessarily focused on the same goals.

ADHDers tend to value independence and freedom over security. That is probably why so many entrepreneurs have ADHD. ADHDers tend to like vocations that have a lot of action and excitement. In addition to entrepreneurs, ADHDers are found in great numbers in careers such as acting, art, music, sales, advertising, teaching, construction and cooking.

This can be particularly difficult in families in which there is another plan for all the offspring. This is common for families in which everyone is a doctor or lawyer or an accountant. There may even be a family business which the seniors would like to pass on to the next generation. It just may not be a good fit for an ADHD adult. If an ADHD adult is going to be a lawyer for instance, you can bet that will go into criminal law or malpractice or personal injury or any other area where they get to go to court and argue. An ADHDer will not want to do tax law or family law. There is not enough excitement. There is not enough challenge.

Understand also that your ADHD adult will likely consider lifestyles and lifestyle changes fairly rapidly and without much warning. They like to try different things. They're not all that driven by what other people think and are not usually all that worried about fitting in.

Your ADHD adult is also more likely to change jobs frequently. They get bored easily. Routine causes frustration and they look for stimulation elsewhere. They keep looking for a better situation, an ideal situation that gives them maximum freedom and independence. Sometimes they find it in certain kinds of jobs. More often, they try to start their own businesses. Nowadays, they frequently start information businesses on the Internet. There's a lot of stimulation. There's a lot of independence. There is a minimum of oversight or control.

ADHDers frequently do well if they have an extremely organized partner or administrative assistant. ADHDers tend to gravitate toward the creative, content development part of business. They like projects, project development, establishing partnerships, and establishing affiliate relationships. They do not like the day-to-day details of running a business. That is why they need strong administrative support. Remember one of the characteristics of a successful adult with ADHD is the creation of and use of support systems. This is particularly true in business, particularly entrepreneurship.

An ADHD adult will likely have more difficulties sustaining romantic relationships than a neuro-typical adult. There will likely be more marital discord, more separations, more explosive arguments and more divorces than parents would like. Of course, nowadays with the divorce rate being nearly 50%, it's much harder to tell the difference.

Another issue for an ADHD adult is substance abuse. There has pretty much always been fear about starting a child on psychoactive medication at an early age. The fear is that one drug will lead to another drug until they are addicted. This is the often mentioned but totally unproven gateway effect. That is, you start them on this drug, they'll naturally go to other drugs. In fact, the ADHDers who are treated early with medication are less likely to have later drug problems than those who had ADHD but were not treated with medication.

ADHDers treated early and consistently throughout life are indeed less likely to have drug problems later in life. However, they still have ADHD and they still crave new experiences. Plus, like everyone else, they're looking for the perfect solution to all of life's problems. This may lead to a willingness to try new things. I don't know how many times I've been told by an ADHD teenager or young adult that there is nothing like marijuana to make them feel calm and relaxed.

Your child will tend to experiment more with life, try more new things and experiment more with different ways of thinking and behaving, experiment more with different jobs, experiment more with different relationships and experiment more with different lifestyles. They are the children, who as adults, will literally suck all the juice out of life. Some of this is likely to be disturbing. You will find yourself wondering if they are ever going to settle down with one lifestyle, one job, one spouse, one family in one location.

So, your ADHD adult can still cause you some worries even as they approach middle-age. Hopefully, they have developed the skills you've taught them along the way to compensate for their neurologic deficits and live successful, sometimes incredibly successful lives. Hopefully, you get to be the proud parents at your child's graduations, marriages, at the birth of your grandchildren and many other successful milestones in their life.

You have the wisdom to recognize that you need to approach this child differently than your neuro-typical children. You have recognized the need to prepare, plan ahead, analyze your vulnerabilities, and develop your own and your family's routines and traditions to more effectively deal with this child. You have developed your skills in managing, leading and mentoring, so that you can model and teach your child the skills he will need to compensate for his neurologic condition. You have recognized that a behavior modification program, while important, is not enough for an ADHD child. You have learned to be strategic – see the situation, analyze the situation, analyze the people, reinforce all attempts at improvement, model appropriate behavior, find and develop an appropriate support system, and have reasonable expectations.

Here's hoping, that as a result of being a strategic parent, you're getting along better with your child. You're not afraid of your child. You understand his ADHD and how it affects him. Your child gets into less trouble. Your child's grades improve, your home life is more harmonious and your family is happier.

RESOURCES

BOOKS ABOUT ADD/ADHD/LD:

Edward M. Hallowell, M.D.
Driven to Distraction
Answers to Distraction
Delivered from Distraction
Superparenting for ADD

Thomas Phelan, Ph.D.
1-2-3 Magic
All about Attention Deficit Disorder
Surviving Your Adolescents

Mel Levine
The Myth of Laziness
A Mind at a Time

Russell Barkley
Attention Deficit Hyperactivity Disorder
Taking Charge of ADHD
ADHD and the Nature of Self-control
Your Defiant Child

Timothy Wilens, M.D.
Straight Talk about Psychiatric Medications for Kids

Winifred Anderson, et al
Negotiating the Special Education Maze

Blake E.S. Taylor
ADHD and Me
Peter & Pamela Wright
Special Education Law
From Emotions to Advocacy

Kenny Handelman
Attention Difference Disorder

ADD / LD Websites:

www.terrygingrasphd.com

www.additudemag.com

www.myadhd.com

www.help4adhd.org

www.chadd.org

www.ldonline.org

www.allkindsofminds.org

www.pbs.org/wgbh/misunderstoodminds

www.ldsuccess.org

www.frostig.org

www.wrightslaw.com

www.advocacyinstitute.org

www.ldanatl.org

www.ld.org

www.cec.sped.org

AUTHOR
DR. TERRY JAMES GINGRAS

As a clinical psychologist who thought he knew a fair amount about parenting, Dr. Terry Gingras had much to learn from his ADHD child. He was an adult psychologist. He did not treat children. As a result, he didn't know how to help his own son, but he learned. He went from knowing little about ADHD to diagnosing and treating it as a major part of his practice.

After 30 years of experience raising his own ADHD child successfully and working with hundreds of ADHD children and their families, Dr. Gingras has created an effective 5 step plan to raising a productive and happy ADHD adult while enjoying the process much more along the way.

This is the first book in a series of books that will help parents of ADHD children to raise not only a happier child but a more responsible adult.

www.ADHDStrategicParenting.com

Made in the USA
Middletown, DE
14 August 2017